The Evolution of Illustration

by Claudia Mareis & Reinhard Wendler

Like the two issues that preceded it, this third volume of *Illusive* gathers together an international selection of contemporary positions in illustration, thereby providing an overview of current developments within the field. Illustrations from both commercial and artistic contexts have been compiled in order to overcome the strict distinction between commercial and artistic illustration and thus to open up fresh possibilities for extending the virulent debate about contemporary art and design in a productive direction.

The collection of work in this book makes no claim to be complete. The intention is rather to present international positions of outstanding quality in an overview that makes them accessible and easier to evaluate. The collection is supplemented by interviews with various illustrators who provide interesting and at times surprising insights into the working methods, techniques and motivation involved in their art and design. This means that alongside the extensive collection of images to be found in this publication, there is also an examination of the actual conditions of illustrative work and the contexts of contemporary illustration.

The design of model books

An artist of the late Middle Ages such as Villard d'Honnecourt, would identify the three *Illusive* volumes as *model books[1]*. The master builder from the 13th century travelled around a Central Europe that was largely influenced by the new Gothic style and collected architectural, sculptural and pictorial works in the form of sketches. Once captured on paper, these brand new forms of design expression could easily be sent on travels of their own and consequently they spread out across Europe. Thus in a certain sense, Villard

performed a similar task to the one that the publishers of this volume saw themselves confronting. It comes as no great surprise, then, to discover that works separated by centuries adhere to almost identical design principles. In both the present volume and the medieval model books, we have several images collected onto one page. In both cases, there is no (or hardly any) text providing reference to the particular context from which an image was taken. And in both cases, this design principle has its own rationale and its specific productivity.

Normally, an illustration does not stand as an isolated entity. It illustrates something else. It accompanies some content—generally in the form of a text—and supports the transmission of that content's information. Yet it never remains passive in relation to the textual content. Rather, it provides an interpretation, a commentary, emphasising certain aspects and ignoring others. In this way, text and illustration merge to become what is a single unified medium in its own right—a so-called iconotext[2] whose meaning is nonetheless formed by its two components.

If one takes the illustrations out of their particular contexts and places them in direct juxtaposition to one another—as has been done on the pages of *Illusive*—then the unity of the iconotext is broken back down and a new context dominated by images is created from the visual elements. Within the fresh semantic context of a tableau[3], new or different aspects of the various illustrations attract our attention. For example, recent developments in illustration become strikingly apparent where they had previously remained invisible, scattered as they were over hundreds of publications in all manner of different fields. In this volume, two clear trends come to light: the marginalisation of vector graphics in favour of an intense engagement with the materiality of illustrations, and the emergence of retro styles oriented towards the period between the World Wars and before the First World War.

From digital to material — and back

In his essay *From material to digital and back*[4], the design theorist Gui Bonsiepe describes how material-based design practices and techniques are changing in accordance with digital technologies — and in the other direction, how digital interaction has a specific relationship with manual activities and material presentations. A similarly reciprocal interplay between materiality and digital media can also be observed in contemporary illustration. Over the last few years, there have been signs of a shift in attention away from vector-based illustrations towards looser handmade works. The trend towards the *material* and *manual* aspects of illustration is clearly recognisable in this publication of *Illusive:* rather than subjecting an image to precise digital vectorisation, illustrations are increasingly produced by hand with rough scribbles, paper cut-outs or freely sketched outlines in pencil, felt-tip and biro. Instead of working with digital paths and templates, people are reaching once again for the scissors and glue, the paper and sticky tape. But what becomes equally apparent is that neither the *material* nor the *manual* are to be found in their pure form in the illustrations. In their place we discover a complex interweaving of computer-aided and manual practices and techniques, of digital and analogue image processes. In other words, the material has asserted itself on numerous levels in the form of the digital, and vice versa[5].

Illustrations conceived along these lines occupy a significant position in the volume at hand. Their appeal lies in this hybrid and sometimes irritating interdependence between digital technology and artistic craftsmanship. For example, one series features exotic-looking animal and landscape illustrations in the form of delicate paper reliefs (pp. 90 – 93), while another incorporates lettering into floral patterns in a complex manner (pp. 94 / 95). Two more series present black silhouette work that is either unusually fine or starkly reduced (p. 88 and pp. 104 / 105), with both types deriving their aesthetic appeal from a paper materiality that has remained visible due to the shadow effect. A further series shows netlike lattice structures that depict dreamy floral motifs — gnarled trees, wild flowers, climbing plants and delicate birds (p. 89). Although the precision and complexity of such reliefs is evocative of sophisticated handcraft, one can also detect traces of a digital aesthetic that still appears to exert its influence even when it has been most radically abandoned. In a variation of the now almost innumerable adaptations of the digital using other media, one series imitates digital pixel images (pp. 110 / 111) by creating different colour gradings with the help of brown adhesive tape in layers of varying opacity. The outcome is a fascinating combination of digital aesthetic and handmade creation in an image. But regardless of whether digital technologies or aesthetics are actively involved in creating such illustrations — as final artwork in their various publications, they all display the form of digitalised image reproduction. The aesthetic look of the illustrations may change as a result, but their hybrid appeal remains unbroken — if not actually more intense.

The new as revaluation of the old

The stylistic effects of displacement and superimposition can be found in the illustrations that embrace retro styles from the interwar and pre-First World War period, revitalising them for the aesthetic concerns of the 21st century. Noteworthy here is a series of largely black-and-white photo collages (pp. 240/241) that assimilate representations of the female body from contemporary fashion magazines while at the same time recalling the historical photo collages and movement studies of different artistic avant-gardes within modernism—Dadaism and Surrealism in particular. Similarities between the historical and the contemporary photo collages are displayed in the way they both employ cutting-edge image processing technologies to present the human body as a visually deconstructible object. In the period of the artistic avant-garde at the beginning of the 20th century, the production of this grotesque and surrealist kind of *hyperreality* was still performed by multiple superimposition and the manual collaging of photographs[6], while the same effects can now be achieved using transparent overlays and multiple digital Photoshop layers as well as gently contoured masks and transitions. And although the results originate from eras separated in time, the similarities and references are not restricted to the aesthetic and stylistic level. Despite or perhaps even because of the different approaches that were and are used in their production, they highlight a technologically and visually manipulated image of the body that is capable of opening up the discussion about standardised bodily ideals and their visual mass-media dissemination through the medium of the picture. Another series in this volume not only borrows stylistic elements from the photo collages of the artistic

avant-garde but goes on to blend them with pictorial stereotypes from fashion photography of the 1950s and 1960s as well as the fluorescent-coloured, geometrically abstract formal language of the 1980s (p. 238/239). Fragmented images of women's faces appear on backgrounds in pastel shades of citrus, apricot and pistachio—as if the only way for something *new* to arise in the eclectic and aesthetic mixture of these illustrations are through a reassessment and revisualisation of the established, the outdated and the historical. These kinds of compositions based on conventional visual formulae reflect the view of the cultural theorist Boris Groys, whereby the new should not be regarded as something *absolutely new* but as a process of revaluation within existing cultural hierarchies and values: *The innovation lies in revaluing the worth of what one has always seen and known*[7].

If you examine the colour, composition and narrative aspects of some of the works in this book's master chapter and compare them with examples of young figurative art[8], you notice a remarkable similarity in how current trends in illustration and contemporary art draw on older styles and visual traditions. These parallels highlight the way in which visual themes now circulate between art and design, how current developments in the field of illustration are intensely connected with those in art, and how art and design questions can no longer be contained within boundaries that used to be virtually impregnable. One concrete impact of this development is that artists and illustrators no longer position their work solely within the context of their own discipline but will often ascribe their work to the *other* side: artists work as illustrators and illustrators open up spaces in which they can produce art. This is another factor in explaining why the works are so similar.

This publication enables the aesthetic and therefore cultural processes of revaluation, innovation and evolution in the field of illustration to be presented on a visual level and placed in relation to one another, thus generating opportunities for comparison. The fact that this extensive, if admittedly incomplete collection—this *model book* of contemporary illustration—has now been compiled for the third time, allows it to provide a well-founded visual overview of and insight into the fascinating breadth of contemporary illustration and its development in recent years.

1   Scheller, Robert W.: Exemplum. Model—Book Drawing and the Practice of Artistic Transmission in the Middle Ages (ca. 900—ca. 1470). Amsterdam. 1995.

2   On the concept of the iconotext: Wagner, Peter: Reading Iconotexts. From Swift to the French Revolution, London 1995; Wagner, Peter: Introduction: Ekphrasis, Iconotexts, and Intermediality—the State(s) of the Art(s). In: Wagner, Peter (ed.): Icons—Text—Iconotext. Essays on Ekphrasis and Intermediality. Berlin / New York. 1996, pp. 1—40.

3   Established as a method of cultural science by Aby Warburg, cf. Warnke, Martin; Brink, Claudia (ed.): Der Bilderatlas Mnemosyne. Berlin. 2000.

4   Bonsiepe, Gui: Design: Von Material zu Digital und zurück. In: Bonsiepe, Gui: Interface. Design neu begreifen. Mannheim. 1996.

5   Pratschke, Margarete et al.: Digitale Form. Bildwelten des Wissens. Kunsthistorisches Jahrbuch für Bildkritik. Vol. 3.2. Berlin. 2005, p. 8.

6   Cowan, Michael; Sicks, Kai Marcel: Leibhaftige Moderne. Körper in Kunst und Massenmedien 1918 bis 1933. Bielefeld. 2005, p. 365ff.

7   Groys, Boris: Über das Neue. Versuch einer Kulturökonomie. Frankfurt a. Main. 2004, p. 14.

8   cf. Robert Klanten, Hendrik Hellige, Sven Ehmann, Pedro Alonzo (eds.): The Upset. Young Contemporary Art. Berlin. 2008.

Content

Naïve & Basic

Naively serious in their approach—and absolutely untouched by irony—the illustrations in this chapter might not be true to scale or life, but they are certainly true to their creators' interpretation of the world around them.

Pared down, yet by no means purist, they thrive on playful reduction: on the bare minimum of strokes, shapes and patterns and on deliberate omission, to distil their subject's vital essence, the spirit of what is portrayed. To this end, some might re-explore the youthful nostalgia and pure, unspoilt figures, patterns and colour schemes of their own upbringing, yet over the course of the last few years both artists and artwork have grown up—at least a little.

Underneath the wealth of drips and blobs, of sprinkles, speckles and analogue scratches, lurks a strong desire for straightforward authenticity, coupled with meticulous skill. Do not be fooled by their light-hearted touch—although some might seem a little rough around the edges, these images cherish their imperfections as a speck of humanity in an all-too-perfect world. And their creators, too, do their best to forget about preconceived rules and techniques, yet retain an astute sense of style and aesthetics.

And here is where their formal training comes in—like kids on an egg hunt, they pick and mix from a plethora of traditional illustration techniques: here, overprinting, silk-screen aesthetics, Op Art patterns, linocuts, textile design and classic typography make friends with a touch of folklore and naïve exotica. Stir in a plethora of geometric shapes, a dash of Kandinsky and the classic mid-20th century colour palette, and you get a contemporary take on Modernism that pays homage to the genre's icons, from Saul Bass to Charlie Harper.

By capturing the unspoilt optimism of post-war US design and advertising—where the promise of never-ending economic growth and a fridge/car/air conditioner for every household made anything seem possible—these artists fill in the blanks between the lines of their own colouring books to conjure up something from nothing: the unfiltered delight of (re)discovery.

Scotty Reifsnyder

Title: Rugged Stud
(Young at Heart poster series)
Format: Poster
Technique: Drawing, digital
2007

Scotty Reifsnyder

Title: White Rabbit
(Young at Heart poster series)
(top left)
Format: Poster
Technique: Drawing, digital
2007

Title: Kinky Cat
(Young at Heart poster series)
(top right)
Format: Poster
Technique: Drawing, digital
2007

A. Micah Smith

Title: Jenny Lewis /
The Elected Poster
(bottom left)
Client: MySpace Music
Format: Poster
Technique: Drawing, digital
2006

Title: Gomez
(bottom right)
Client: Gomez
Format: Poster
Technique: Drawing, digital
2006

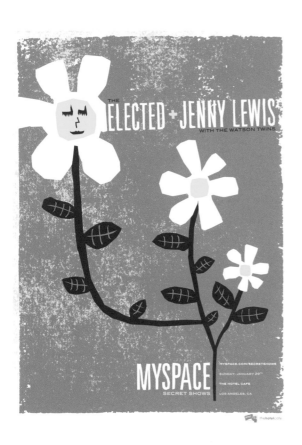

Scotty Reifsnyder

Title: Don Peris Holiday Show
Client: Musician Don Peris
Format: Poster
Technique: Drawing, digital
2008

Orlando Hoetzel

Title: Höhenflug
All Images:
Technique: Ink, digital
2006

Borja Bonaque

Title: City
All Images:
Technique: Digital
2009

Interview Pietari Posti

Just the right blend of Nordic cool and Mediterranean ease, it was love that brought Pietari Posti to Barcelona—and the second big passion of his life: illustration. In his work, Posti presents the metropolis not as a looming, crumbling behemoth, but filled with wide-eyed joy, hope and desire. His GIANTS! in the city, for example, might find themselves lost in the urban jungle, yet view their surroundings with friendly astonishment. Caught between the flow of traffic, it is up to us to fill in the blanks between the Finn's fluid strokes, held together by naïve curiosity.

Background

I was born in Helsinki, Finland, in 1979 and now live and work in Barcelona. After graduating from Lahti Polytechnic with a BA in graphic design, I moved to Spain in 2005 to become a professional illustrator. Don't get me wrong—I do like graphic design, but drawing and illustration has always been my true love. For a welcome change from the editorials that still make up the bulk of my work, I also do illustrations for advertising, merchandising and apparel such as T-shirts, wallets or furniture.

Inspiration and influences

I don't think growing up in Finland has left too much of a mark on my work—only Tove Jansson, the creator of everyone's childhood favourites, the Moomins, comes to mind . Comics like Asterix and Tintin were far more influential. I remember creating my own Asterix character—even before I could read! This was followed by a Marvel and DC comics period. At some point, I was convinced that I would crack the superhero comic industry and create the next Hellboy, but my drawings never quite made the cut. After that, I moved on to underground graphic novels by Manara, Crumb, Moebius et al. and manga classics like Akira. Nowadays, I draw inspiration from a healthy mix of comics, graphic design, Japanese woodcuts and vintage illustrations. Lately, I have also been digging a lot of fine artists like Egon Schiele, Murakami or Andy Warhol.

Skills and techniques

Besides my background in graphic design, I have always drawn a lot; I have been doodling in the corners of pages since I was a mere four years old. In school, illustration was not on the schedule, so I am more or less self-taught. At some point, I started to experiment with colouring my illustrations in Photoshop and soon fell in love with the overall ease and simplicity of the process. Although my illustrations are seventy per cent Photoshop, I want to avoid the digital look, so I add a lot of handmade textures, stains and similar "accidents" to the picture. In a way, my arrangement of colours and lines in separate layers resembles a digital silk-screening process. The only difference: the digital version is far more flexible—and you can always resort to Ctrl+Z.

Work and play

These images show a mix of editorial work and more personal projects. While I do not say no to money, l have been fortunate enough to be able to say no to projects that do not excite me professionally. I love the fact that illustration is and can be used on a huge range of materials and surfaces and that it has found its way onto new products like furniture. It is great when illustration becomes part of something so physical and long-lived!

John Lennon once said: "A career is what happens when you're making other plans." I love the fact that I never know exactly what I will do in the upcoming months, who I might collaborate with or where in the world my work will appear … but after many years of doing just that I could look back and call it a career.

Pietari Posti

Title: GIANTS! — Deer
Format: Poster
Technique: Mixed media
2008

Pietari Posti

Title: GIANTS! — Niña
(top left)
Format: Poster
Technique: Mixed media
2008

Title: Circus
(top right)
Client: American Express / VSA
Format: Book illustration
Technique: Mixed media
2009

Title: She
(bottom)
Client: Muze Magazine
Format: Editorial
Technique: Photoshop
2009

Pietari Posti

Title: Storm
(top)
Client: Fortune Magazine
Format: Editorial
Technique: Mixed media
2009

Title: Infinity
(centre)
Format: Poster
Technique: Mixed media
2008

Title: Architecture Meets Fashion
(bottom left)
Client: J'N'C Magazine
Format: Editorial
Technique: Mixed media
2008

Title: Great Expectations
(bottom right)
Client: Best Life
Format: Editorial
Technique: Mixed media
2008

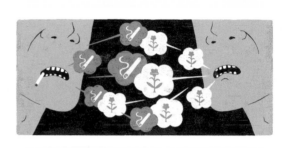

Jens Bonnke

Title: Glasses
(top left)
Client: Märkische Allgemeine
Format: Editorial
Technique: Mixed media
2009

Title: Smokers Vs. Non-Smokers
(top upper right)
Client:
Süddeutsche Zeitung Magazin
Art Director: Ludwig Wendt
Format: Editorial
Technique: Mixed media
2008

Title: Duty Free
(top lower right)
Client:
Süddeutsche Zeitung Magazin
Art Director: Ludwig Wendt
Format: Editorial
Technique: Mixed media
2008

Title: Chair
(bottom left)
Client: Märkische Allgemeine
Format: Editorial
Technique: Mixed media
2009

Title: Yps Primeval Crabs
(bottom centre)
Client: Rowohlt Verlag
Format: Editorial
Technique: Mixed media
2009

Untitled
(bottom upper right)
Client: GeldIdee Magazin
Credits:
Format: Editorial
Technique: Mixed media
2008

Untitled
(bottom lower right)
Client: Süddeutsche Zeitung
Magazin
Art Director: Daniel Bognar
Format: Editorial
Technique: Mixed media
2008

Jens Bonnke

Title: Poisoned
(top upper left)
Client:
Süddeutsche Zeitung Magazin
Art Director: Daniel Bognar
Format: Editorial
Technique: Mixed media
2008

Title: Bitter Pills
(top lower left)
Client:
Süddeutsche Zeitung Magazin
Art Director: Ludwig Wendt
Format: Editorial
Technique: Mixed media
2007

Title: Park Bench
(top right)
Client: Märkische Allgemeine
Format: Editorial
Technique: Mixed Media
2009

Untitled
(bottom left)
Client: KircherBurkhardt
Art Director: Tana Budde
Format: Editorial
Technique: Mixed media
2007

Untitled
(bottom right)
Client: GeldIdee Magazin
Format: Editorial
Technique: Mixed media
2008

Yuki

Title: Wedding of Elitza
Concept / Drawing:
Maki Shimizu
Wood cutting / Printing:
Yuko Chikazawa
Format: Limited print
Technique:
Woodblock printing
2008

Yuki

Title: Vanessa
(top left)

Title: Maki Shimizu
(top right)

Title: Oliver Gibbins
(bottom left)

Title: Masashi Togami
(bottom right)

Concept / Drawing *(all)*:
Maki Shimizu
Wood cutting / Printing *(all)*:
Yuko Chikazawa
Format *(all)*: Limited print
Technique *(all)*:
Woodblock printing
2008

Andrew Bannecker

Title: Sale Amour Boy
(top left)
Technique: Digital
2008

Title: Sale Amour Girl
(top right)
Technique: Digital
2008

Untitled
(bottom)
Client: Boston Globe
Format: Editorial
Technique: Digital
2009

Andrew Bannecker

Title: Tears of Hope
(top left)
Gallery: Manifest Hope DC
Technique: Digital
2008

Title: Lost at Sea
(top right)
Technique: Digital
2008

Title: Life and Death
(bottom)
Technique: Digital
2009

LA VERDAD OCULTA

Sue Walker

El REENCUENTRO

Sue Walker

FURIA

G.M. Ford

Cristóbal Schmal

Title: Verdad Oculta
(The Hidden True)
(top left)
Client: El anden
Format: Editorial
Technique: Hand-drawn,
linocut, digital
2009

Title: El Reencuentro
(The Reunion)
(top right)
Client: El anden
Format: Editorial
Technique: Hand-drawn,
linocut, digital
2008

Title: Furia (Rage)
(bottom left)
Client: El Anden
Format: Editorial
Technique: Hand-drawn,
linocut, digital
2008

Title: Paris Smells
(centre right)
Client: Ling Magazine
Format: Editorial
Technique: Hand-drawn,
linocut, digital
2009

Title: Ana & Pavlik
(bottom right)
Format: Wedding invitation
Technique: Hand-drawn,
linocut, digital
2009

Cristóbal Schmal

Title: Siren
(top left)
Client: Poolga
Format: Ipod/iphone wallpaper
Technique: Hand-drawn,
linocut, digital
2009

Title: Man
(top right)
Client: Printastic
Format: Poster
Technique: Hand-drawn,
linocut, digital
2009

Title: Trio
(bottom left)
Client: Printastic
Format: Poster
Technique: Hand-drawn,
linocut, digital
2009

Title: The Wolf
(centre right)
Technique: Hand-drawn,
linocut, digital
2009

Title: Kein Schöner Land
(bottom right)
Client: Das Magazin
Technique: Hand-drawn,
linocut, digital
2009

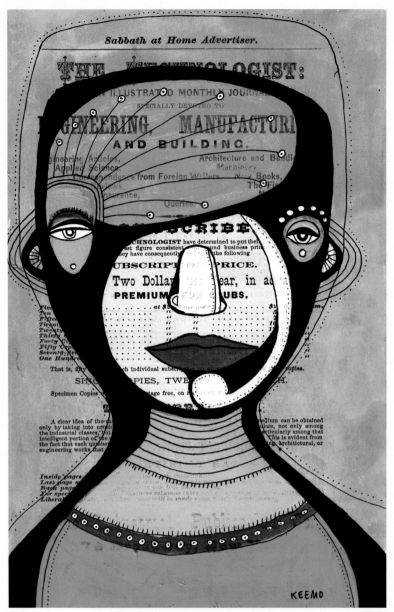

Title: Insert Chicken and Egg
Reference Here
(top left)
Client: Private collector
Format: Exhibition
Technique: Acrylic,
watercolour and ink
2009

Title: The King
(top right)
Client: United Ambient Media AG
Format: Postcard
Technique: Watercolour and ink
2009

Title: At the Intersection of
Money and Hope, Series #3
(bottom)
Client: Private Collector
Format: Exhibition
Technique: Acrylic,
watercolour and ink
2009

Title: The Business Is More of
an Art Than The Art is a Business
(top left)
Client: Private collector
Format: Exhibition
Technique: Watercolour and ink
2009

Title: Still a Possiblity. #3
(top right)
Client: Private collector
Format: Exhibition
Technique:
Acrylic and ink on wood
2009

Title: Half of My life Has Been
Spent With Her
(bottom left)
Client: Private collector
Format: Exhibition
Technique: Acrylic and ink
2009

Title: I Know We Have All Felt
This Way
(bottom right)
Client: Private collector
Format: Exhibition
Technique: Watercolour, ink
2008

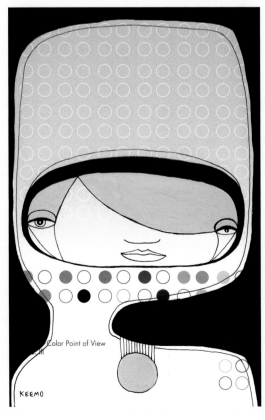

Ana Albero

Title: Tuberculosis,
Psoriasis, Obesity
All images:
Format: Part of graduation work
Technique: Pencil drawing,
digital colouring
2008

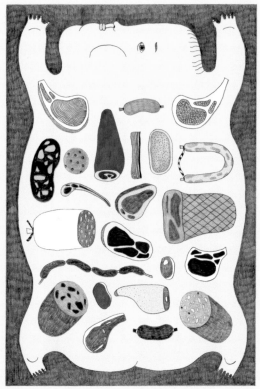

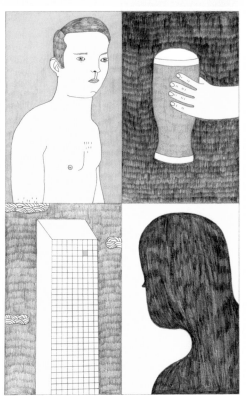

Stuart Kolakovic

Title: Beard Tales
(top left)
Client: Tight Fit zine
Format: Editorial
Technique: Mixed media
2008

Untitled
(top right)
Client: Rotopol Press
Format: Exhibition
Technique: Mixed media
2008

Title: Worship Something
(bottom left)
Client: Tiny Showcase
Format: Exhibition
Technique: Mixed media
2008

Title: Postcard
(bottom right)
Format: Self-promotion
Technique: Mixed media
2008

Matte Stephens

Title: Boston
(top)
Technique: Gouache on plywood
2008

Title: Portland
(bottom left)
Technique: Gouache on plywood
2008

Title: Uncle Rutherford
gives the kids a lift
(right top)
Technique: Gouache on plywood
2008

Title: Augustus the lion
(right bottom)
Technique: Gouache on plywood
2008

Matte Stephens

Title: Family Vacation
(top)
Technique: Gouache on plywood
2008

Title: New Orleans
(bottom)
Technique: Gouache on plywood
2008

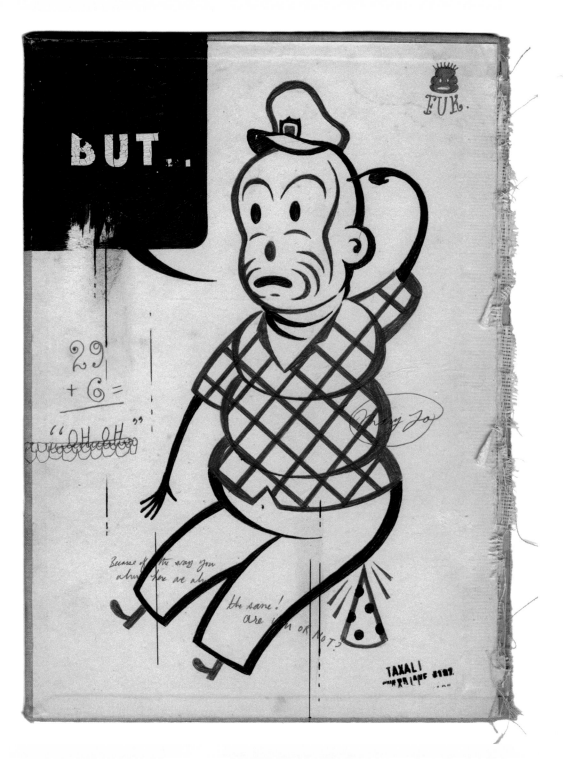

Gary Taxali

Title: But...
(top)
Client: Corey Helford Gallery
Format: Exhibition
Technique: Hand-drawn
2008

Title: Yo-Yo Fun
(bottom left)
Client: Jonathan LeVine Gallery
Format: Exhibition
Technique: Silkscreen
2009

Title: Fussly
(bottom right)
Client: Jonathan LeVine Gallery
Format: Exhibition
Technique: Hand-drawn
2009

Gary Taxali

Title: I'm On It
(top)
Client: Magic Pony Gallery,
Format: Exhibition
Technique: Hand-drawn
2007

Title: Eddie Martini's
(bottom left)
Client: Eddie Martini's Restaurant
Format: Promotional
Technique: Hand-drawn,
silkscreen
2009

Title: Yoga
(bottom right)
Client: Entertainment Weekly
Format: Editorial
Technique: Silkscreen
2008

Paul Thurlby

Title: Illustrated Letters
All Images:
Technique: Photoshop
2009

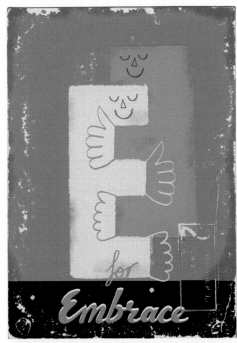

Paul Thurlby

Title: Illustrated Letters
Technique: Photoshop
2009

Christopher Nielsen

Title: Vacant Lot
(top left)
Format: Exhibition
Technique: Acrylic
2009

Title: Born
(top right)
Client: Born Magazine
Art director: Scott Benish
Format: Web
Technique: Acrylic
2008

Title: Mauled
(bottom left)
Client: Plansponsor
Art Director: SooJin Buzelli
Format: Editorial
Technique: Acrylic
2009

Title: Compass
(bottom right)
Client: Plansponsor
Art Director: SooJin Buzelli
Format: Editorial
Technique: Acrylic
2009

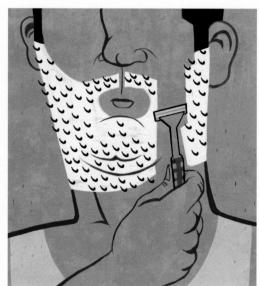

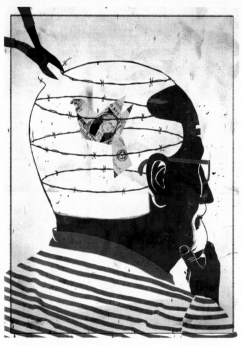

Emiliano Ponzi

Title: Spanking
(top left)
Client: Milk magazine, France
Art Director: Louise Desrosiers
Format: Editorial
Technique: Digital
2008

Title: Shaving commas
(top right)
Client: Rcs publishing, Italy
Art director: Gloria Ghisi
Format: Editorial
Technique: Digital
2008

Title: Saving money
(bottom left)
Client:
Financial Planning magazine
Art Director: James Jarnot
Format: Magazine cover
Technique: Digital
2009

Title: The Minefield Ahead
(bottom right)
Client: Time UK
Art director: Paul Mumby
Format: Editorial
Technique: Digital
2008

Emiliano Ponzi

Title: Conceptual Portrait
of Charles Bukowski
(top left)
Technique: Digital
2008

Title: American Style
(top right)
Client: Newsweek
Art Director: Patty Alvarez
Format: Magazine full page
Technique: Digital
2008

Burka
(bottom left)
Technique: Digital
2008

Pretending
(bottom right)
Client: Businessweek
Art director: Don Besom
Technique: Digital
2009

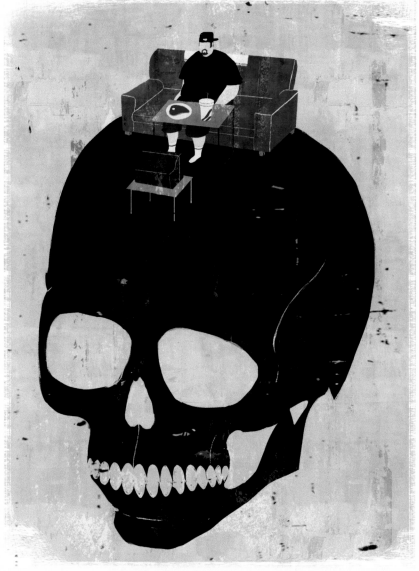

Mocchi Mocchi

Untitled
(top)
Format: Greeting card
Technique: Silkscreen
2007/8

Title: Flowers Blossoming
(bottom left)
Client: The Art Group
Format: Poster
Technique: Silkscreen
2007/8

Untitled
(bottom right)
Format: Exhibition
Technique: Silkscreen
2009

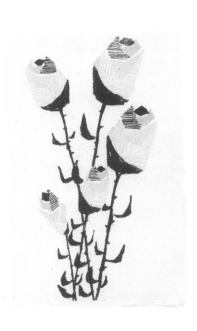

Mocchi Mocchi

Untitled
(top)
Format: Greeting card
Technique: Silkscreen
2008/9

Title: With the Wind
(bottom left)
Client: The Art Group
Format: Poster
Technique: Silkscreen
2007/8

Title: Journey Into the Distance
(bottom right)
Client: The Art Group
Format: Poster
Technique: Silkscreen
2007/8

Mocchi Mocchi

Title: Tree
(top left)
Format: Exhibition
Technique: Silkscreen
2007/8

Untitled
(top right)
Client:
Woodmansterne Publications Ltd.
Format: Greeting card
Technique: Silkscreen
2008/9

Untitled
(bottom)
Client: Vision track
Format: Exhibition
Technique: Silkscreen
2009

Mocchi Mocchi

Untitled
(top left)
Client:
Woodmansterne Publications Ltd.
Format: Greeting card
Technique: Silkscreen
2008/9

Title: Sound in forest
(top right)
Format: Exhibition
Technique: Silkscreen
2007/8

Untitled
(bottom)
Client:
Watashi no Heya Living Co., Ltd.
Format: Greeting card
Technique: Silkscreen
2007/8

Julia Guther

Title: Butcher The Bar
(top)
Client: Morr Music
Format: Record sleeve
Technique: Watercolour, digital
2008

Title: Balloon Ride
(bottom left)
Client: Morr Music
Format: Tour poster
Technique:
Watercolour, oil pastels, pencil
2009

Title: The Wooden Birds
(bottom right)
Client: Morr Music
Format: Record sleeve
Technique: Watercolour
2009

Julia Guther

Title: Pisces
(top)
Client: Maxi
Format: Editorial
Technique: Watercolour, digital
2008

Title: September Compilation
(bottom left)
Client: Eardrums
Format: Record sleeve
Technique: Oil pastels, pencil
2008

Title: Music Shoppers Live Longer
(bottom right)
Client: Morr Music
Format: Poster and bag
Technique: Oil pastels, pencil
2008

Irana Doue*

Untitled
All images
Technique: Acrylic on paper*
2009

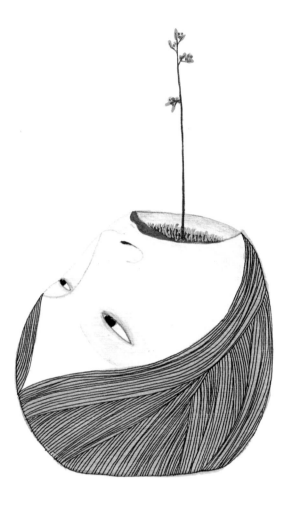

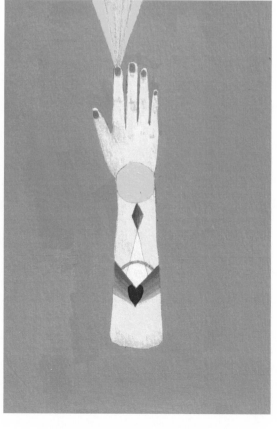

Silja Goetz

Title: Intelligence series
All images:
Client: Cosmopolitan Germany
Art Director: Angela Hüppe
Format: Editorial
Technique:
Collage, pencil, Photoshop
2008

Julia Pfaller

Title: Bavarian Series
All Images:
Format: Personal piece
Technique: Linoprint
2009

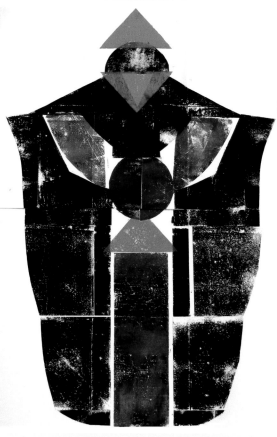

Julia Pfaller

Title: Sindbad
All Images:
Client: Die Gestalten Verlag
Format: Book illustration
Technique: Mixed media
2005

Andrew Holder

Title: Mountain Town
(top left)
Technique: Mixed media
2009

Title: Mahishasura
(top right)
Technique: Mixed media
2009

Daniel Stolle

Title: Waterfall
(bottom left)
Client: SZ Wissen
Art Director: Thomas Kartsolis
Format: Editorial
Technique: Digital
2009

Title: Pyramid
(bottom right)
Client: Luomurinki Finland
Format: Editorial
Technique: Digital
2009

Maija Louekari

Title: Dadel
(left)
Client: Marimekko
Format: Textile print
Technique: Hand-drawn,
papercut
2007

Title: Nuppu
(bottom right)
Client: Marimekko
Format: Textile print
Technique: Hand-drawn,
papercut
2007

Andrew Holder

Title: Royalty
(top right)
Technique: Mixed media
2009

Monika Aichele

Title: How to Make Snow
(top left)
Format: Postcard
Technique: Silkscreen
2007/2008

Title: This Must Be the Place
(top right)
Client: New York Times
Art Director: Nicholas Blechman
Format: Editorial
Technique: Mixed media
2008

Title: Icemother
(bottom left)
Client: The New York Times
Art Director: Nicholas Blechman
Format: Editorial
Technique: Vector drawing
2007

Title: Orang-Utan
(bottom right)
Client: Office Mareike Dittmer
Art Director: Mareike Dittmer
Format: Postcard
Technique: Silkscreen
2008

Christopher Nielsen

Title: Don't Panic
(top left)
Client: Don't Panic
Art Director: Anik Labreigne
Format: Advertising
Technique: Acrylic
2008

Ilja Karsikas

Title: Too Much to Swallow
(top right)
Client:
Helsinki University Bulletin
Format: Editorial
Technique: Ink, Photoshop
2008

Title: Finnish Genetics
(bottom left)
Client:
Helsinki University Bulletin
Format: Editorial
Technique: Ink, Photoshop
2009

Title: The Mystery of
the Capricious Brain
(bottom right)
Client:
Helsinki University Bulletin
Format: Editorial
Technique: Ink, Photoshop
2008

Nate Williams

Title: Lion Dress
(top left)
Technique: Digital
2008

Title: Horses & Lions
(top right)
Format: Pattern
Technique: Digital
2009

Title: Letter Life
(bottom left)
Format: Pattern
Technique: Digital
2009

Title: Laughter
(bottom right)
Format: Pattern
Technique: Digital
2009

Nate Williams

Title: Women
(top left)
Format: Pattern
Technique: Digital
2009

Title: Berlin
(top right)
Client: City of Berlin
Format: Postcard
Technique: Digital
2008

Title: Beautiful Life
(bottom left)
Format: Silkscreen poster
Technique: Digital
2008

Title: Grad School
(bottom right)
Format: Pattern
Technique: Digital
2009

Simon Wild

Title: Typewriter God
(top left)

Title: Halldor
(top right)

Title: Rugby Coach
(bottom left)

Title: Dive Number 5
(bottom centre)

Title: Tired Eyes
(bottom right)

Format: Editorial
Technique: Hand-drawn,
collage, Photoshop
2009

Paul Wearing

Title: New Season
(top left)
Client: PW Art Limited
Format: Limited Edition Print
Technique: Digital
2008

Title: Forever in the Landscape 2
(top right)
Client: PW Art Limited
Format: Limited Edition Print
Technique: Digital
2009

Title: Genetic Research
(bottom)
Client:
Cedars Sinai Medical Center
Art Director: Doug Joseph
Format: Advertising
Technique: Digital
2008

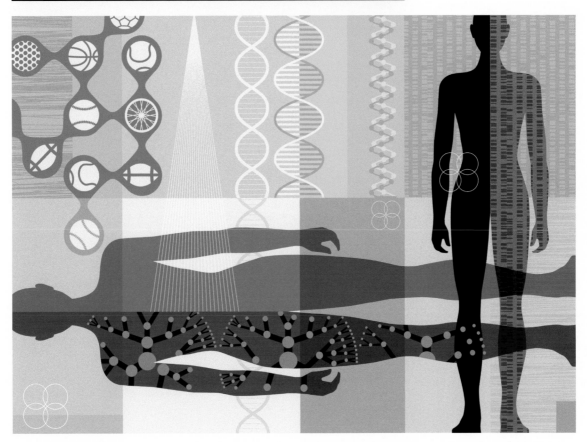

Laura Ljungkvist

Title: Kitchen
(top)
Technique: Photoshop
2009

Title: Vases
(bottom left)
Technique: Ink on paper,
Photoshop
2009

Title: 3 Chairs
(bottom right)
Technique: Ink on paper,
Photoshop
2008

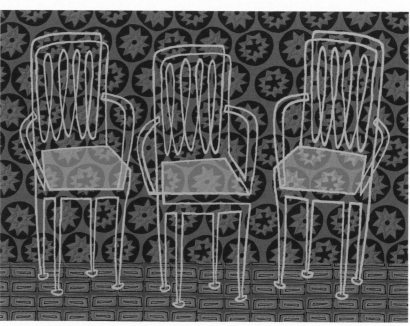

Paul Wearing

Title: Hand & Globe
(top)
Client: United Airlines
Agency: Fallon, Minneapolis
Format: Advertsing
Technique: Digital

Title: Acute Care for
Sick Children
(bottom left)
Client: Cedars Sinai
Medical Center
Art Director: Doug Joseph
Format: Advertising (Fundraising)
Technique: Digital
2008

2006 Title: What You Think
(bottom right)
Client: Telegraph Magazine
Art Director: Gary Cochran
Format: Editorial
Technique: Digital
2007

Maria Eva Mastrogiulio

Title: Gatito
(top left)
Technique: Mixed media
2008

Title: The Whale
(bottom left & top bottom right)
Format: Children's book
Technique: Mixed media
2008

Mike Dornseif

Title: Diamonds for Tigers
(top left)
Technique: Digital
2009

Title: Elephant Gem
(top right)
Technique: Digital
2009

Title: Everthing I Am
(bottom left)
Technique: Digital
2009

Maria Eva Mastrogiulio

Title: The Whale
(bottom right)
Format: Children's book
Technique: Mixed media
2008

EVERYTHING I AM

Herr Hell

Title: Fnuk Ya!
All images:
Format: Book illustration
Technique: Ink, digital
2009

Herr Hell

Title: The Little Snail
(diverse images)
Format: Book illustration
Technique: Ink, digital
2009

Cecilie Ellefsen

Title: January
(top)
Client: Commando Group
Format: Calendar illustration
Technique: Digital
2007

Title: In the Forest Deep
(bottom left)
Format: Exhibition promo card
Technique: Digital
2009

Untitled
(bottom right — 2 images)
Technique: Digital
2008

Hans Baltzer

Title: Lobster
(top left)
Format: Screen print Poster
Technique: Hand-drawn, digital
2008

Title: Big Beetle
(top right)
Format: Screen print Postcard
Technique: Hand-drawn, digital
2008

Judith Drews

Title: Imagination
(bottom left)
Client: Familienwelt, Hamburg
Format: Editorial
Technique: Hand-drawn, digital
2008

Title: Carly
(bottom right)
Format: Children's cardboard
book
Technique: Hand-drawn, digital
2008

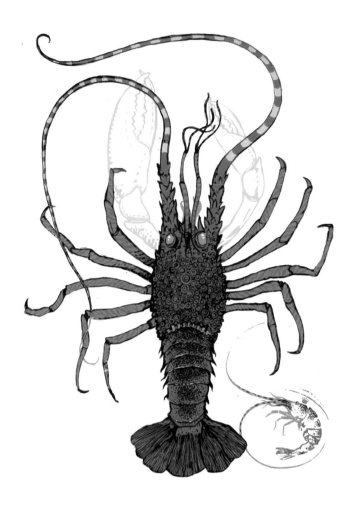

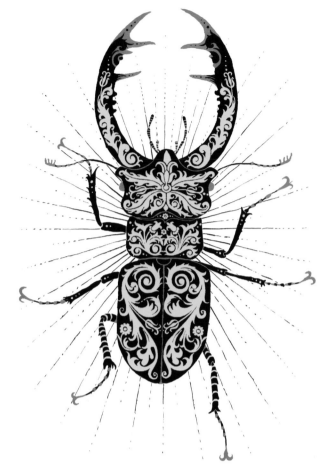

Anke Weckmann

Title: Branches
(top left)
Technique: Ink, digital
2009

Title: Scissors
(top right)
Technique: Ink, digital
2008

Title: Blue Birds
(centre left)
Client: Red Cap Cards
Format: Greeting card
Technique: Ink, digital
2008

Title: Shoes
(centre right)
Technique: Ink, digital
2008

Title: Cassiopeia Cat
(bottom)
Technique: Ink, digital
2008

Laura Varsky

Title: Piripipí
(top left)
Technique: Ink, digital
2006

Title: 08
(top right)
Technique: Ink, digital
2008

Title: Dorothy
(bottom left)
Client: Gata Flora Magazine
Format: Editorial
Technique: Ink, digital
2008

Title: Bird
(centre right)
Client: Fenchurch
Format: Textile
Technique: Ink, digital
2007

Title: Dorothy's Flowers
(bottom)
Client: Gata Flora Magazine
Format: Editorial
Technique: Ink, digital
2008

Alice Stevenson

Title: The Night Visitor
(top)
Technique: Silkscreen 2007

Title: World
(bottom upper left)
Client: World of Interiors
Format: Editiorial
Technique: Drawing, Photoshop
2007

Title: Sensory Perception
(bottom lower left)
Technique: Drawing, Photoshop
2005

Title: Card
(bottom right)
Client: Art Angels
Format: Greeting card
Technique: Drawing, Photoshop
2007

Alice Stevenson

Title: Vodafone
(top)
Client: Vodafone, Brand Union,
Format: Packaging
Technique: Drawing, Photoshop,
2008

Title: Londonfields
(bottom left)
Technique: Watercolour on paper
2009

Title: Structure of Reality
(bottom right)
Technique: Drawing, Photoshop
2005

Madeleine Stamer

Title: Girl from Takadanobaba
(top left)
Technique: Hand-drawn, brush,
Gauche, watercolour
2007

Title: Come Ride With Me #2
(top right)
Technique: Hand-drawn,
brush, ink
2008

Title: Birds Are Both Beautiful
and Fascinating
(bottom left)
Technique: Hand-drawn,
brush, ink
2007

Title: Wake Up Sleepy
(bottom right)
Technique: Hand-drawn, brush,
ink, gouache, charcoal
2007

Madeleine Stamer

Title: Black Swan
(top left)
Technique: Hand-drawn,
brush, ink
2009

Title: Welcome
(top right)
Technique: Hand-drawn,
brush, ink, gouache
2008

Title: 3
(bottom left)
Technique: Hand-drawn,
brush, ink
2008

Title: Microeca Leucophaea
(bottom right)
Technique: Hand-drawn, brush,
ink, gouache, watercolour
2007

Francesco D'Isa

Title: Beauty is Overrated
(top)
Client: Bigfatfanny
Model: Medea
Technique: Cintic graphic tablet,
Photoshop
2009

Title: Reality Bites
(bottom)
Client: Pornsaints
Model: Porn star Athena Hollow
Format: Print on canvas
Technique: Cintic graphic tablet,
Photoshop
2009

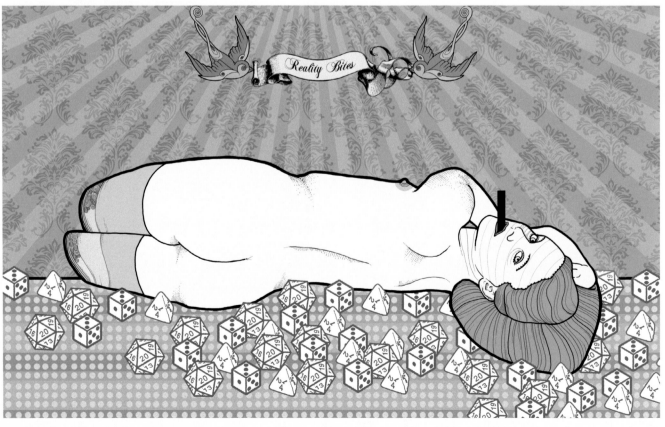

Francesco D'Isa

Title: Eden
(top)
Technique: Cintic graphic tablet,
Photoshop
2009

Title: Fly Away
(bottom left)
Client: Bigfatfanny
Technique: Ink on paper
2006

Title: Incomprehension
(bottom right)
Model: Ermione
Technique: Hand-drawn,
Photoshop
2008

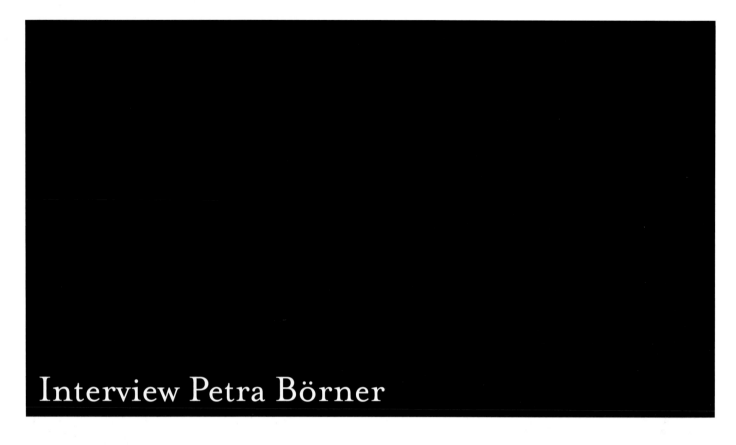

Interview Petra Börner

Versatile Scandinavian export Petra Börner weaves evocative patterns and striking prints from a wealth of organic inspirations. Since graduating from London's Central Saint Martins College, Börner has been spreading her linocut-inspired illustrations and designs to textile patterns for Cacharel, Louis Vuitton and her own label, Rosetta, as well as book covers, editorials and interior design.

Background

I never once considered a profession outside of art or design. My great-grandfather was quite an inventor and he liked to photograph and paint his family and surroundings—I remember drawing from his paintings as a child. From a very young age, I spent most of my time making clothes and textiles, drawing, painting, saving up for art supplies or looking for objects to be used for projects and installations. Although I have trained in fashion, design and illustration, my commissions encompass interior design, publishing, editorial, packaging and advertising.

Inspiration and influences

Growing up in the 1970s in Sweden, surrounded by everyday objects designed by the likes of Lisa Larsson, Olle Eksell, Katja of Sweden or Carl Johan De Geer, has definitely left its mark on my work. I grew up in a home where craft and textile art was a family hobby; we would spend most of our summers in the garden experimenting with dyes and fabrics, sewing patterns or tie-dye techniques. After fifteen years "in exile" abroad, my memories of Scandinavia have probably crystallised into a rather romantic concept.

At the same time, I have reached a point where my "handwriting" is truly my own and almost like a real signature, it has become second nature to me. When I set out to draw and view an object, I see a solution in my mind that feels "right". It can be very frustrating to reach this ideal, but it usually works out through repetition.

Skills and techniques

After school, the draw of the big city brought me to London. Here, my studies in fashion, working for other designers and running my own business have really influenced the way I work. I am mostly self-taught and use mixed techniques like drawing, collage, sewing and painting for my simple, graphic compositions.

Work and play

Most of the pieces in this book are excerpts from my sketchbooks, drawn with a ballpoint pen or felt-tip pens.

These drawings were, for the most part, created from memory, away from studio, and serve as a testing ground for new ideas without any pressure or expectation.

It really amazes me how looking at an old work can bring back that particular moment, just like a song. For example, I still remember lying in the grass on a steep point in Cornwall, looking out towards the Atlantic, blue skies and blazing sun above, whilst drawing the graphic horse.

Petra Börner

Title: Magnetic Lady
Format: Exhibition
Technique: Felted pen,
ballpoint pen
2007

Petra Börner

Title: Enchanted Bird
(top left)
Format: Exhibition
Technique: Papercut
2008

Title: Pop Flower
(top right)
Format: Exhibition
Technique: Felt pen,
ballpoint pen
2007

Title : Graphic Hand
(bottom left)
Format: Exhibition
Technique: Felt pen,
ballpoint pen
2007

Title: Graphic Horse
(bottom right)
Format: Exhibition
Technique: Felt pen, ballpoint
pen
2007

Title: John Betjeman Poems
selected by Hugo Williams
(top left)
Client: Faber
Art direction and typography
by Miriam Rosenbloom
Format: Book cover
Technique: Scraperboard
2009

Title: Alice in Wonderland
by Lewis Carroll
(top right)
Client: White's Books
Art direction, colour and
typography by David Pearson
Format: Book cover
Technique: Scraperboard
2009

Title: Sherlock Holmes
by Arthur Conan Doyle
(bottom left)
Client: White's Books
Art direction, colour and
typography by David Pearson
Format: Book cover
Technique: Scraperboard
2009

Title: Pride and Prejudice
by Jane Austen
(bottom right)
Client: White's Books
Art direction, colour and
typography by David Pearson
Format: Book cover
Technique: Scraperboard
2009

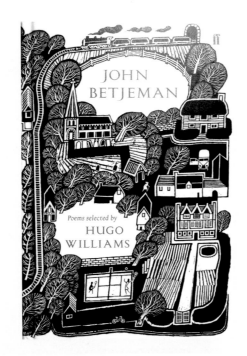

ALICE IN WONDERLAND **W**
LEWIS CARROLL

SHERLOCK HOLMES **W**
ARTHUR CONAN DOYLE

PRIDE AND PREJUDICE **W**
JANE EYRE

Rilla Alexander | Rinzen

Title: Canapy
Client: FSC
(Forest Stewardship Council)
Format: 8 colour calendar
Technique:
Ink and watercolour
2008

The Bungaloo

Title: House No. 20
(top left)
Client: AIGA St. Louis
Technique: Silkscreen
2009

Title: Mogwai
(top right)
Client: Mogwai
Format: Show poster
Technique: Silkscreen
2009

Title: Deer and Birds
(bottom left)
Technique: Silkscreen
2009 / March

Title: Big Business
(bottom centre)
Client: Big Business
Format: Show poster
Technique: Silkscreen
2009

Title: Viking
(bottom right)
Technique: Silkscreen
2009 / May

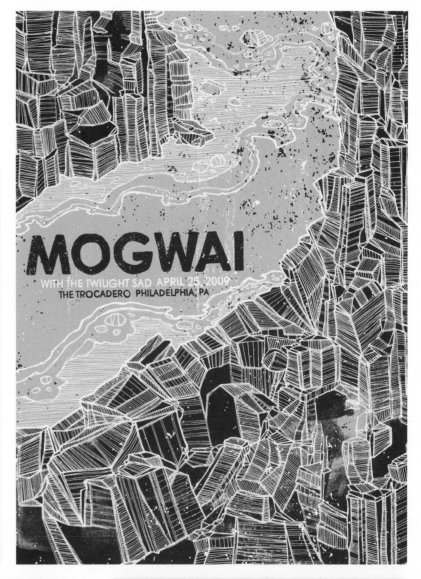

Susan Burghar

Title: Bob Dylan
(top left
Client: Mojo Magazine
Format: Editoria
Technique: Digita
2009

Title: Katy Car
(top right
Client: Katy Car
Format: Record sleev
Technique: Digita
2009

Lehel Kovács

Title: The Lumberjack
(bottom left
Format: Postcard
Technique: Mixed
2008

Title: J.F.K. Eating Spaghetti
(bottom right
Technique: Paintin
2009

Natsko Seki

Title: London
Format: Limited edition print
Technique: Hand-drawn,
collage, Photoshop
2007

Josh Cochran

Title: I Feel Space
(top)
Client: Budweiser / Flavorpill
Art Director:
Jessica Bauer-Greene
Format: Web campaign
Technique: Hand-drawn, digital
2007

Title: The Big Bang
(bottom left)
Client: Las Vegas Life / Pentagram
Art Director: Julie Savasky
Format: Editorial
Technique: Hand-drawn, digital
2007

Title: Clocktower
(bottom right)
Client: Entertainment Weekly
Design Director: Brian Anstey
Format: Editorial
Technique: Hand-drawn, digital
2007

Iris Luckhaus

Title:
Die wunderbare Welt der Lily Lux
(5 images)
Client: Hoffmann & Campe
Co-author: Matthias Klesse
Format: Book
Technique: Digital
2009

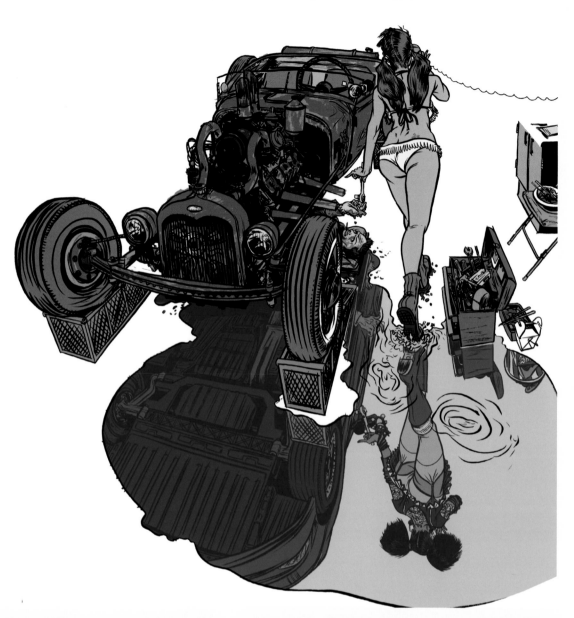

Nathan Fox

Title: Hot Rods
(top)
Client: Complex Magazine
Art Director: Sean B.
Format: Editorial
Technique: Ink, brush, digital
2006

Title: A Clockwork Orange
(bottom left)
Client: Premiere Magazine
Art Director: Dirk Barnett
Format: Editorial
Technique: Ink, brush, digital
2006

Title: Vrrrrmmmm!
(bottom right)
Client: NY Times Magazine
Art Director: Arem Duplesis
Format: Editorial
Technique: Ink, brush, digital
2007

Nathan Fox

Title: Lee Murry
(top)
Client: ESPN magazine
Art Director: Ed Mann
Format: Editorial
Technique: Ink, brush, digital
2008

Title: Exit Interview...
(bottom left)
Client: NY Times Magazine
Art Direction: Cathy Gilmore-
Barnes/Arem Duplesis
Format: Editorial
Technique: Ink, brush, digital
2008

Title: Git' em Kitty...
(bottom right)
Client: Fully of pride—
Kitty Pryde Tribute Show
Curator: Jason Levian
Format: Exhibition
Technique: Ink, brush, digital
2009

Paul Blow

Title: The Judgement Test
(top left)
Client: Radio Times
Credits: Ped Millichamp
Format: Editorial
Technique: Hand-drawn, digital
2009

Title: Stopping the Pedophiles
(top right)
Client: Readers Digest
Credits: Liette Savard
Format: Editorial
Technique: Hand-drawn, digital
2009

Title: Skeel Bros.
(bottom left)
Client: Times—T2
Credits: Alex Bruer
Format: Editorial
Technique: Hand-drawn, digital
2008

Title: Care Home Abuse
(bottom right)
Client: The Independent magazine
Credits: Stephen Petch
Format: Editorial
Technique: Hand-drawn, digital
2009

Tanja Székessy

Title: Robe Plisée
(top)
Technique: Pencil, Photoshop
2009

Title: Garland
(top right)
Format: Exhibition
Technique: Acrylic on canvas
2008

Title: Juggling Balls
(bottom left)
Format: Exhibition
Technique: Acrylic on canvas
2008

Title: Parade
(bottom right)
Format: Exhibition
Technique: Acrylic on canvas
2008

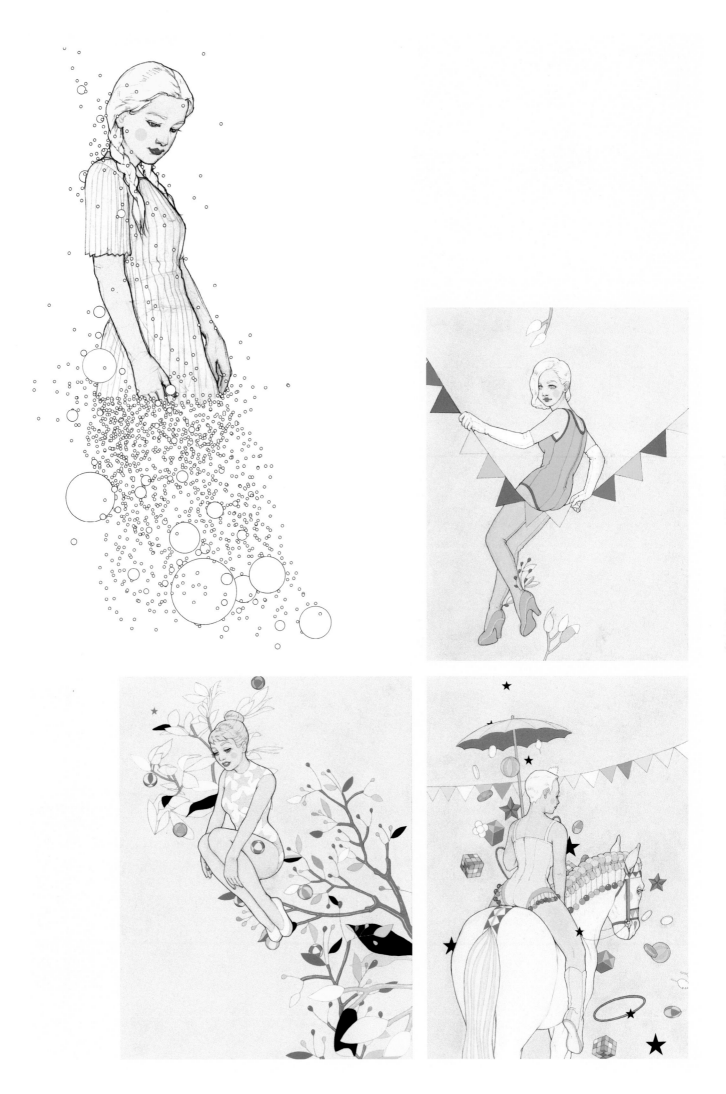

Tactile Illustrations

Who says you need a pen to illustrate? The works assembled in this chapter celebrate the unique immediacy of a physical object—and the process of creation.

Here, a sparkling idea and a few brushstrokes are simply no longer enough: these tactile interventions with a DIY twist escape the confines of their substrate to exploit paper's material properties for a more tangible expression of their creators' style and intent.

While some focus on new angles and folds, others take "cut and paste" back to its origins. In their exploration of the blank page, these "physical illustrators" translate their signature style to objects, sets and scenes that disregard paper's inherent flatness. With just a few tweaks or drops of glue, their basic sheet joins the 3D fold in a redefinition of shape and space.

From the laciest of hand-cut creations—delicate ecosystems, hanging by the finest of threads—to the towering solidity of stucco-like paper murals, these objectified illustrations retrace a history that never was: transposed to novel surroundings, even the abstract and banal gains a new sense of drama and urgency, an immediate "realness" that makes them stand out—by the sheer power of their physical presence.

Incidentally, while paper and board remain the most basic and popular building blocks, there are some notable deviations from the paper trail: look out for layered packing tape in all its pixelated glory or the joy of home-stitched, knitted and crocheted necessities.

Still, there is one thing they all have in common: in order to complete their tour de force, these hands-on artists hand over control to their own creations and succumb to the beauty, effort and exhaustion involved. The reward goes to artist and audience alike: the incredible dedication, the days or months of painstaking work, the desperation of a single wrong cut, all shine through in every single piece.

Blackjune

Title: Tripthychon
Format: Sculpture
Technique: Cut-out
2007

Hina Aoyama

Title: Forest of Heart
(top)

Title: Heron & Heron's head
(bottom left + right)

All images:
Technique:
Paper, scissors
2008

Bovey Lee

Title: Office Tornado
(top)

Title: Atomic Jellyfish
(bottom left)

Title: Little Crimes III
(bottom right)

All images:
Technique:
Chinese rice paper, paper-cut
2007 / 8

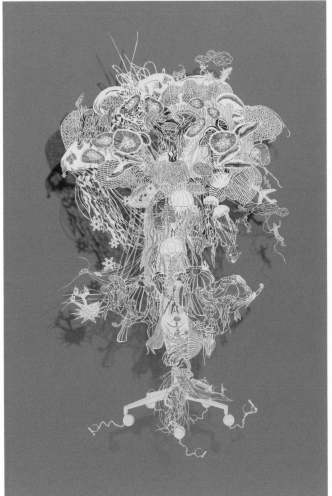

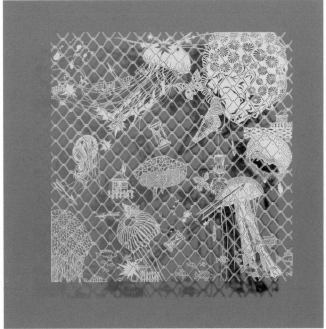

Interview Jeff Nishinaka

Paper sculpture has been around for a good fifty years—and for at least half of this time, Jeff Nishinaka has been one of its main and most popular ambassadors. Born and bred in Los Angeles, Nishinaka slices and shapes his paper reliefs into stucco-like murals that might grow to encompass an entire wall. His tools of the trade: glue and a simple X-Acto knife!

Background

Until college, I did not even know that illustration could be a career. When, in 1979, I was accepted at the Art Center College of Design in Pasadena, I set out to become a serious painter, but discovered paper sculpture instead. Or, should I say, it discovered me! Now, almost 30 years later, I am still an L.A-based illustrator, but in the meantime, I have had numerous exhibitions around the world and even opened an art studio in Japan for a year. At the moment, I am focusing on China, where I recently had an exhibition, or work on private commissions for collectors in Hong Kong and in the USA. It has been a long road—and an interesting one!

Skills and techniques

I have had to learn paper sculpture on my own. There were no classes available. Smooth clean cuts—like the seamless transition from one direction to another in an s-shape—are a vital skill and take lots of practice. You need the entire arm, sometimes the whole body, to make these cuts smooth and flowing. My wrist is always locked in a straight position. Sometimes I even tape my fingers to avoid blisters and use super glue on the cuts …

My tools are very basic: X-Acto knives, French curves, wooden dowels and white glue. No scissors. Keeping everything as simple and basic as possible also makes it easy to travel—although I need the tools for the job, it all boils down to skill and improvisation. Ideas are all important to good work and this can mean a lot of research. Whenever possible, I travel to the actual installation site to gather research and get a better feel for the subject. For example, I have travelled to Africa and China to see and experience the location firsthand. True understanding always makes for a better piece, even in the parts that you do not see.

Inspiration and influences

I am the product of Japanese culture, from my grandparents who came to America in the early 1900s, and of the American culture around me. Although I feel totally American, my paper sculptures have a definite Japanese influence—or so I am told! Of course, any third generation American might feel the same way. The Art Center exposed me to all the great masters, from the Renaissance to Impressionism and Modern Art. Impressionism and Japanese Ukiyo-e woodblock prints were the most influential. In the end, I experiment a lot—looking for new ways to keep my work fresh and energetic, but also timeless and hopefully not trendy.

Work and play

I like choosing projects that pose a challenge. "What have I gotten myself into this time!?" The longest time I have gone without sleep was 43 hours … Staying within my comfort zone is like standing still.

Upping the bar helps me to grow and think outside the box. The project for the main lobby of the ANA Hotel in Tokyo, for example, took three months to complete. I worked with a graphic design studio, a building contractor and a concert lighting designer. The leaf area of the tree was five metres in diameter and the total dimensions of the sculpture were approximately 7 x 7 x 5 metres. In the end, though, I do not have any favourite projects—if anything, I am my own worst critic and always wish I had done at least part of it differently.

Jeff Nishinaka

Title: Sports Hall
Format: Interior wall of the
PSU All-Sports Museum
at Penn State University
Photographer: Ed Ikuta
Technique: Paper hand-cut
with X-Acto knife,
layered, glued
2001

Jeff Nishinaka

Title: El Sereno Phoenix
(top left)
Format: Sculpture for the
main lobby of the Barrio
Action Youth & Family Center
in El Sereno, California
2008

Title: Tiger Mask
(top right)
1997

Title: Downtown Los Angeles
(left centre)
Format: Sculpture for the
main lobby of the Alexan Savoy
Condominium project
2005

Title: Beaver Stadium
(bottom left)
Format: Interior wall of the
PSU All-Sports Museum
at Penn State University
2001

Title: Brooklyn Bridge
(bottom right)
Fotmat: Private commission
1997

All images:
Photographer : Ed Ikuta
Technique: Paper hand-cut
with X-Acto knife,
layered, glued

Jeff Nishinaka

Title: Landmarks of the World
(top left)
Format: Sculpture for permanent
exhibit in the Children's Museum,
East End, Bridgehampton,
New York
2004

Title: Dragon & Phoenix
(top right)
Client: Jackie Chan
Format: Sculpture for the lobby
of Jackie Chan / The JC Group
Main Office, Hong Kong
2006

Title: Preserve
(bottom left)
Format: Sculpture for
Sprint Press, Denver CO
2008

Title: Golden Gate Bridge
(bottom right)
Format: Image used for website
and printed material
2005

All images:
Photographer: Ed Ikuta
Technique : Paper hand-cut
with X-Acto knife,
layered, glued

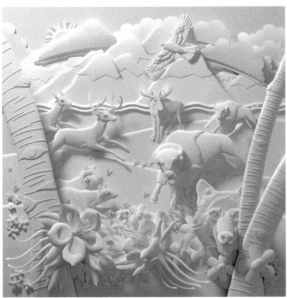

Yulia Brodskaya

Title: Values
(top)
Client: Northlands
Photography: Michael Leznik
Designer: Melissa Hicks
Format: Community report
Technique: Paper quilling
2009

Title: 1000 Songs Everyone Must
Hear (Party Songs & Heartbreak)
(bottom left + right)
Client: The Guardian
Designer: Jeremy Marshall
Art Director: Gavin Brammall
Photographer: Paul Burroughs
Format: Editorial
Technique: Paper quilling
2009

theguardian **The**Observer | 20.03.2009

theguardian **The**Observer | 15.03.2009

Part seven
PARTY SONGS

Part two
HEARTBREAK

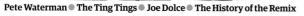

Pete Waterman ● The Ting Tings ● Joe Dolce ● The History of the Remix

Guy Garvey ● Martha Wainwright ● Mariella Frostrup ● Kitty Empire

Yulia Brodskaya

Title: Eww
(top)
Client: o.b. Canada
Photographer: Michael Leznik
Art Director: Patrick Shing
Format: Poster
Technique: Paper quilling
2009

Title: Terreus 100% Suomi
(bottom left)
Client: Tervakoski
Photography: Michael Leznik
Creative Director: Pekka
Nokelainen
Format: Poster
Technique: Paper quilling
2009

Title: Ran Out of Ideas, Now
What?
(bottom right)
Photography: Michael Leznik
Technique: Paper quilling
2008

Helen Musselwhite

Title: Owl Party
(top)
Technique: Papers and wallpaper
hand-cut with a scalpel, layered
with foam board
2008

Title: Little Fox
(bottom left)
Technique: Paper hand-cut with a
scalpel, layered with foam board
2008

Helen Musselwhite

Title: Sage Stag
(top)
Technique: Painted paper, watercolour, paper hand-cut with a scalpel, layered with foam board
2009

Title: Home Sweet Home
(bottom left)
Technique: Paper hand-cut with a scalpel, layered with foam board
2009

Title: We Are Family
(bottom right)
Technique: Paper hand-cut with a scalpel, layered with foam board
2009

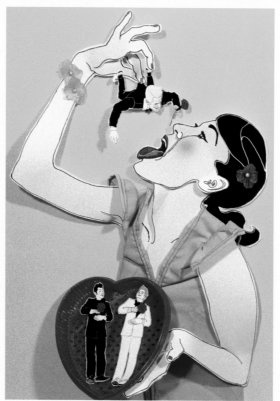

Ingela och V

Title: Paper Dolls and Jeweller
(top lef
Client: Marie Lavae
Format: Exhibition piec
Technique: Illustration, collag
200

Title: Rosie Gets Dresse
(top righ
Technique: Illustration, Collag
200

Title: Face O
(bottom left
Technique: Illustration, Collag
2006

Title: Maneate
Client: Showroom Enformsal
(bottom right
Format: Exhibition piec
Technique: Illustration, collage
2006

Angela och Vi

Title: The City Can Eat You Up
(top left)
Technique: Illustration, collage
2009

Title: Stuck in a Fairytale
(bottom left)
Client: 2 agenten
Format: Editorial
Technique: Illustration, collage
2008

Title: Volume Mascara
(bottom right)
Client: Urban Outfitters
Format: Exhibition piece
Technique: Illustration, collage
2007

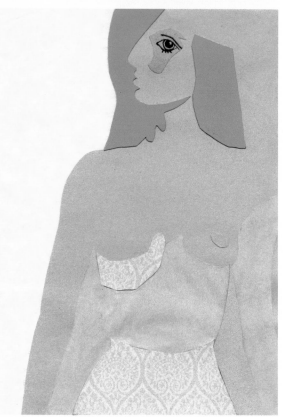

Evelina Bratell

Title: Ms Sour
(top left)
Technique: Scalpel, glue, pencil,
hole-puncher, Tipp-Ex, collage
2009

Title: With Title
(top right)
Technique:
Scissor, scalpel, glue, collage
2007

Title: Ms Sweet
(bottom left)
Technique: Scissor, scalpel, glue,
pen, Tipp-Ex, wallpaper, paper
2009

Title: Jane Doe I
(bottom right)
Technique:
Scissor, scalpel, glue
2005

Christian Tagliavini

Title: Dame di Cartone/
Cubism III
(top left)

Title: Dame di Cartone/
17th Century II
(top right)

Title: Dame di Cartone/
Cubism II
(bottom left)

Title: Dame di Cartone/
17th Century I
(bottom right)

All images:
Technique: Cardboard, glue,
oil, acrylic
2008

Bela Borsod

Title: Gir
(top left, bottom left + right,
Client: Tatle
Format: Editoria
Technique: Paper installatio
2008

Title: Alto Profilo
(top right,
Client: Elle Italy
Format: Editoria
Technique: Paper installatio
2008

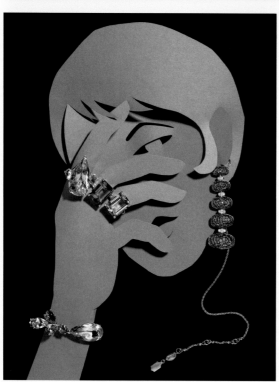

Bela Borsodi

Title: Alto Profilo
All images:
Client: Elle Italy
Format: Editorial
Technique: Paper installation
2008

Jenny Grigg

Title: Ernest Hemingway
"Death in the Afternoon"
(top left)

Title: Ernest Hemingway
"The Old Man and the Sea"
(top right)

Title: Ernest Hemingway
"A Moveable Feast"
(bottom left)

Title: Ernest Hemingway
"Garden of Eden"
(bottom right)

All images:
Client: Lindhardt og Ringhof
Format: Book cover
Technique: Paper, scalpel
2008

Jenny Grigg

Title: Ernest Hemingway
"The Sun Also Rises"
(top left)

Title: Ernest Hemingway
"The Green Hills of Africa"
(top right)

Title: Ernest Hemingway
"Dangerous Summer"
(bottom left)

Title: Ernest Hemingway "Over
the River and into the Trees"
(bottom right)

All images:
Client: Lindhardt og Ringhof
Format: Book cover
Technique: Paper, scalpel
2008

Esther Gebauer

Title: Mariposas
(top left)
Technique: Hand-sewn

Title: Me
(top right)
Technique: Sewing
2009

Title: Florecita
(bottom right)
Technique: Hand-sewn
2008

Clemens Habicht

Title: Superannuation Squirrels
(bottom left)
Client: Bulletin Magazine,
Sydney Australia
Format: Editorial
Technique: Cut paper collage
2007

Caroline Hwang

Title: July, May
(top left, bottom left)
Client: Starbucks Taiwan
Format: Illustration for a
monthly planner
Technique: Painting, sewing
2007

Title: Quiet Moments of
a Party Girl
(top right)
Client: 826CHI
Art Director: Cody Hudson
Format: Book illustration
Technique: Painting, sewing,
collage
2008

Title: Disabled: Please Don't Fight
It. Its Always the Same.
(bottom right)
Technique: Painting, sewing
2007

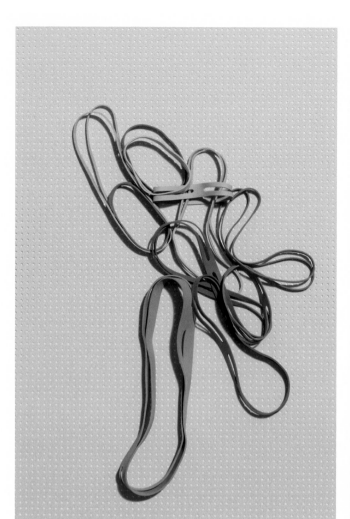
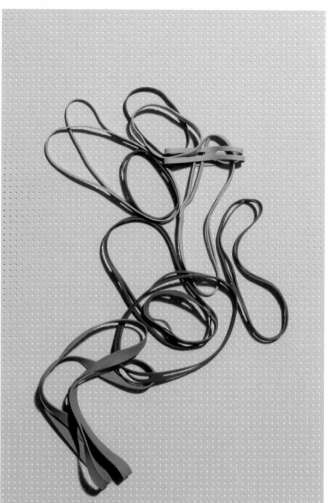

Frank Hülsbömer

Title: Tales of Clusters and
Bubbles
Technique: Collage
2009

Sarah Illenberger

Title: Ingredients for
Chilli con Carne Recipe
Photographer: Ragnar Schmuck
Technique: Scalpel, scissors,
glue, folding, hole punch,
foil paper, circle cutter,
tissue paper, cardboard
2008

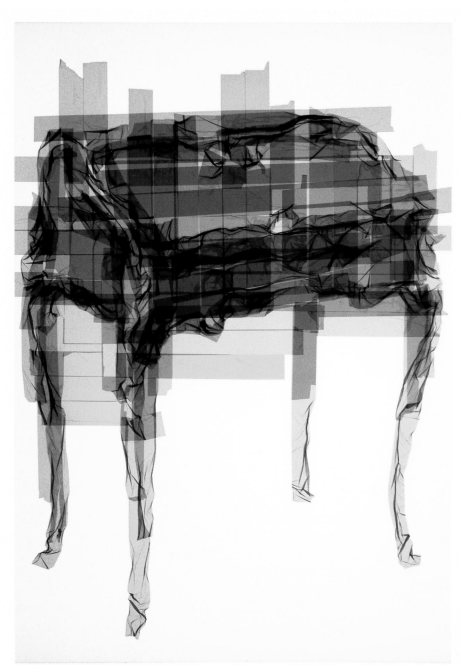

Mark Khaisman

Title: $293,300 in 1996
(top left)

Title: Frame_8
(top right)

Title: Lara and Abby
(bottom left)

Title: Frame_5
(bottom right)

All images:
Technique:
Packaging tape in Plexiglas
2007

Mark Khaisman

Title: Frame_7
(top left)

Title: $86,980 in 1995
(top right)

Title: Emily, Arielle and Helen
(bottom right)

Title: Frame_13
(bottom left)

All images:
Technique:
Packaging tape on Plexiglas
2007 / 8

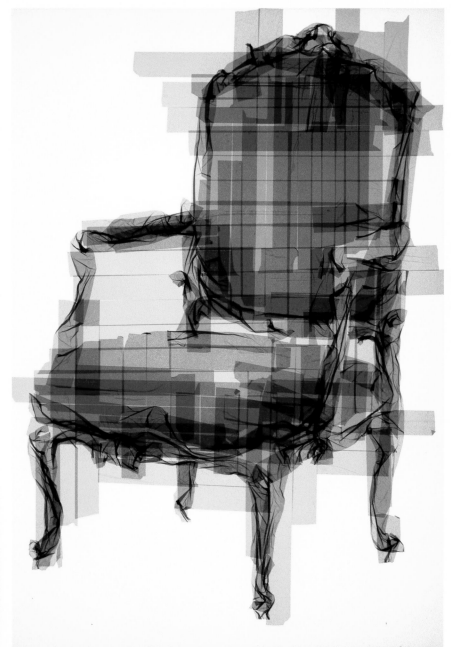

Fashion

If fashion designers are the enemies of women, as many long-suffering style-victims claim, then illustrators are their sharpest sword: they seduce us with an unattainable ideal; a towering, slender five-stroke goddess, clothed in an effortless style less suited to the average hopeful. By selling this promise of unattainable glamour, fashion can flatter or reveal glaring flaws, enhance or hide our personality. At the same time, it thrives on appropriation, on mixing and matching and sly references—no one copies more beautifully!

Thus tasked with the role of fixing a brief moment in time, the latest fleeting fancy of our collective fashion consciousness, the illustrator has to seduce within seconds to communicate the gist of a style. In their subordinate role as mere backdrop and canvas, his drawn or sketched "dummies" serve as faceless placeholders for the latest model.

Well, all this has changed. Fashion is no longer about selling textiles, but the mere promise of a better life: one of youth, beauty, style and originality. While customers might slip on a dress to slip into character, the new breed of fashion illustrators focus on the character the designers want to dress.

All of a sudden, their "models" have a face—and plenty of sass. Fully formed personalities in their own right, they are no longer bland empty vessels, but confident blueprints of girls we would love to meet. Here, meek and subdued simply won't do—a bit of drama, from doe-eyed damsel to sharp-shouldered vixen, from stark austerity to floaty innocence, adds spice to the overall fashion experience, enhanced by the medium's liberal use of stylish exaggeration.

To this end, illustrators dip deep into their box of tools and techniques, blending soft watercolours and accidental splashes with angular 1920s decadence, untouchable "Great Gatsby" glam, the unadulterated "come hither" sensuality of voluptuous 1950s pin-ups and even the odd sideways nod to the sharp-nipped pencils of Otto Dix or George Grosz. While some shapes and patterns go over the edge to escape their own boundaries, others take a more literal approach and stitch their ideals with thread or wool in yet another iteration of immaculate craftsmanship.

What remains is the task of selling a promise, an illusion that conveys more than reality, more than a photo could ever achieve. And although many designers and artists are male, on paper this remains the domain of women, fashion's favourite canvas and captive audience.

Naja Conrad-Hansen

Title: Red
Client: Bleed, Epos card, Visa
Technique: Oil on linen
2008

Stina Persson

Title: Addolorata e Consolata
(top – 2 images)
Format: Exhibition
"Immacolata and her Friends"
Technique: Ink, watercolour,
paper collage
2007

Title: Violetta
(bottom left)
Format: Exhibition
"Immacolata and her Friends"
Technique: Ink, watercolour,
paper collage
2007

Title: Iben Ho
(bottom right)
Client: Iben Ho
Format: Editorial stylebook
Technique: Ink, watercolour,
papel picado, tissue paper,
Photoshop
2007

Stina Persson

Title: Annunziata
Format: Exhibition
"Immacolata and her Friends"
Technique: Watercolour, paper
collage and papel picado
2007

Untitled
(top left)
Client: Isetan
Format: Catalogue cover
Technique:
Watercolour, ink, Photoshop
2008

Untitled
(top right)
Client: Bloomingdale's
Format: Advertising
Technique:
Watercolour, ink, Photoshop
2007

Untitled
(bottom left)
Client: Saks Fifth Avenue
Format: Invitation
Technique:
Watercolour, ink, Photoshop
2005

Untitled
(bottom right)
Client: Neiman Marcus
Format: Invitation
Technique:
Watercolour, ink, Photoshop
2006

Kareem Iliya

Untitled
(top left)
Technique:
Watercolour, ink, Photoshop
2007

Untitled
(top right)
Client: Isetan
Technique:
Watercolour, ink, Photoshop
2008

Untitled
(bottom left)
Client: H & M
Technique:
Watercolour, ink, Photoshop
2003

Untitled
(bottom right)
Client: The New York Times
Sunday Magazine
Format: Editorial
Technique:
Watercolour, ink, Photoshop
2008

Tina Berning

Title: Lady, Lady 1—4
All images:
Format: Exhibition
Technique: Mixed media
2008

Tina Berning

Title: Artificial Volume
(top left)
Client: Branche & Business
Fachverlag
Fashion Director:
Marita Sonnenberg
Format: Editorial
Technique: Mixed media
2008

Title: Top In Doing The Job
(top right)
Client: Playboy Germany
Format: Editorial
Technique: Mixed media
2007

Title: Women's World,
Feminine Aesthetics
(bottom left)
Client: Branche & Business
Fachverlag
Fashion Director:
Marita Sonnenberg
Format: Editorial
Technique: Mixed media
2008

Title: Tease, please
(bottom right)
Client: Glow Magazine
Format: Editorial
Technique: Mixed media
2007

Anja Kroencke

Title: Happy Winte
All images
Client: Nippon Vogue / Japar
Format: Advertoria
Technique: Mixed medi
2008

Lesja Chernish

Title: Androgyny
(top left)
Technique: Mixed media
2008

Title: Kewie
(top right)
Technique: Mixed media
2008

Title: Yarn
(bottom left)
Technique: Mixed media
2008

Untitled
(bottom right)
Technique: Mixed media
2007

Lesja Chernish

Title: Anna
(top)
Technique: Mixed media
2008

Title: Dark Venus
(bottom left)
Technique: Mixed media
2008

Title: Cookie Jar
(bottom right)
Technique: Mixed media
2008

Lesja Chernish

Title: Behind
Technique: Mixed media
2008

Margot Mace

Title: Am
(top left

Title: Frid
(top right

Title: Duba
(bottom left

Title: Yuk
(bottom right

All images
Client: Clarin
Format: Publicit
Technique
Watercolour, ink per
2008/9

Margot Macé

Title: Pearl
(top left)

Title: June
(top right)

Title: St Honoré
(bottom left)

Title: Madame K
(bottom right)

All images:
Client: Clarins
Format: Publicity
Technique:
Watercolour, ink pen
2008/9

Margot Mace

Title: Hai
Client: Clarin
Format: PR imag
Technique: Watercolour, ink pe
2006

Title: Tokyo
Client: Magazin officiel japos
Format: Editoria
Technique: Watercolour, ink pe
2006

Naja Conrad-Hansen

Title: Rock Me Amadeus
Client: Grafuc
Technique: Ink
pencil, Photoshop
2006

Margot Macé

Title:
I Must Be In a Good Place Now
(top left)

Title: Itsu-ka
(top right)

Title: Gossip
(bottom left)

Title: Cocktail
(bottom right)

All images:
Client: Exhibition Barbizon
Technique : Ink on linen
2009

David Despau

Title: Su
(top)
Technique: Pen, ballpoint pen,
ink, Photoshop
2008

Title: Yellow
(bottom left)
Technique: Pen, ballpoint pen,
ink, Photoshop
2008

Title: Mondofreak
(bottom right)
Client: Lamilk magazine
Format: Editorial
Technique: Pen, ballpoint pen,
ink, Photoshop
2008

David Despau

Title: Cate
(top left)
Technique: Pen, ballpoint pen,
ink, Photoshop
2008

Title: Calva
(bottom left)
Technique: Pen, ballpoint pen,
ink, Photoshop
2008

Title: Beauty
(bottom right)
Technique: Pen, ballpoint pen,
ink, Photoshop
2008

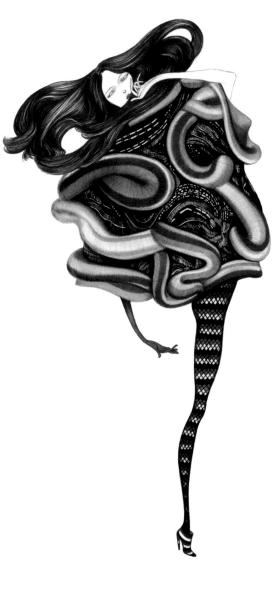

Laura Lain

Title: Kenz
(top lef
Client: I.T. Post magazin
Format: Editoria
Technique: Hand-draw
200

Title: Tiger of Swede
(top righ
Client: +4
Format: Poste
Technique: Hand-draw
200

Title: Comme des Garçon
(bottom lef
Technique: Hand-draw
200

Title: Rad Houran
(bottom right
Client: Rad Houran
Technique: Hand-draw
200

Laura Laine

Title: Gareth Pugh
(top left)
Client: I.T. Post magazine
Format: Editorial
Technique: Hand-drawn
2008

Title: Rad Hourani
(top right)
Client: Rad Hourani
Technique: Hand-drawn
2009

Title: Lolita
(bottom left)
Client: Welcome To Finland
Format: Editorial
Technique: Hand-drawn
2008

Title: Viktor & Rolf
(bottom right)
Client: I.T. Post magazine
Format: Editorial
Technique: Hand-drawn
2008

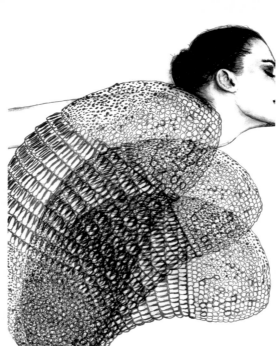

Sabine Pieper

Untitled
(top left)
Technique: Hand-drawn
2009

Untitled
(top right)
Technique: Mixed media
2009

Untitled
(bottom left)
Technique: Mixed media
2009

Title: Armadillo
(bottom right)
Technique: Hand-drawn
2009

Sabine Pieper

Title: Interrelation 4
(top — 2 images)
Technique: Mixed media
2009

Title: Army Of Me
(bottom left)
Technique: Mixed media
2009

Untitled
(bottom right)
Technique: Mixed media
2009

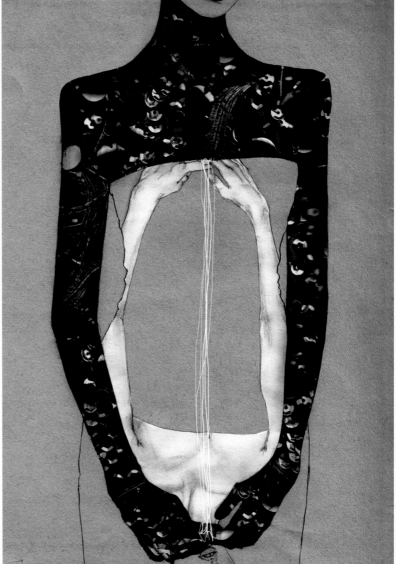

Lina Bodén

Title: Dorotea
(top left)
Technique: Hand-drawn, digital
2008

Title: Ester
(top right)
Technique: Hand-drawn, digital
2008

Title: Alter/Mode
(left centre)
Client: Alter/Mode
Format: Editorial
Technique: Hand-drawn, digital
2008

Title: +46 Fashion
(bottom left)
Client: ODD Projects
Format: Print
Technique: Hand-drawn, digital
2009

Title: Sigrid
(bottom right)
Technique: Hand-drawn, digital
2008

Loreto Binvignat Streeter

Title:
Mala hierba nunca muere I, II, III
(top 3 images)
Client: Bigoteprimerizo
Format: Print
Technique:
Pencil, watercolour, Photoshop
2008

Lina Bodén

Title: Katinka
(bottom 2 images)
Credits: Ruvan Wijesooriya
Technique: Hand-drawn, digital
2008

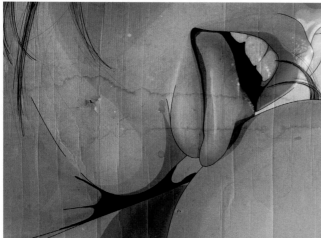

In

Title: Mia
(top,

Title: Lui
(bottom upper left,

Title: Jooo
(bottom lower left,

Title: Amin
(bottom right,

All images
Format: Exhibition
Technique : Digital drawing
2008

ni

Title: Zoe
(top)
Format: Exhibition

Title: Sunsone
(bottom lower left)
Format: Exhibition

Title: Twosuns
(bottom upper right)
Format: Exhibition

Title: Nylon 1 + 2
(bottom upper left,
bottom lower right)
Client: Gudberg magazine
Format: Editorial

All images:
Technique: Digital drawing
2008

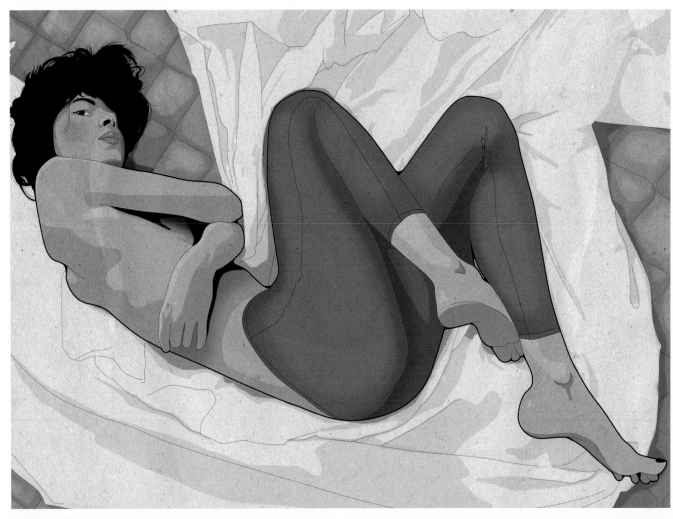

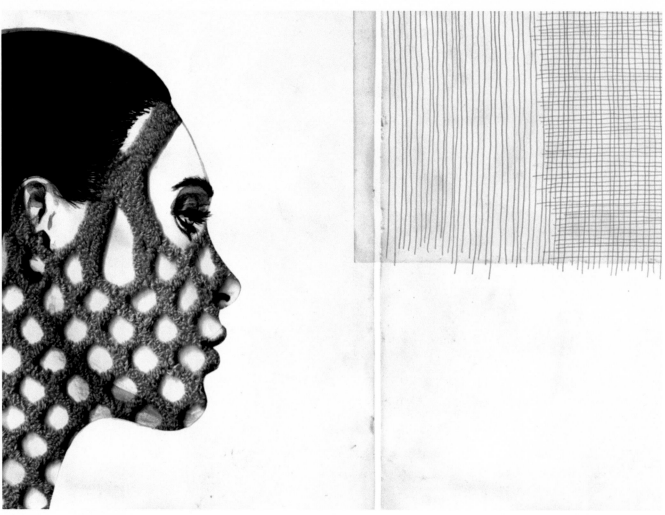

Sabine Pieper

Title: Discipline
(top)
Technique: Mixed media
2009

Untitled
(bottom left)
Technique: Mixed media
2009

Untitled
(bottom right)
Title: I Quiet Myself I
Technique: Mixed media
2008

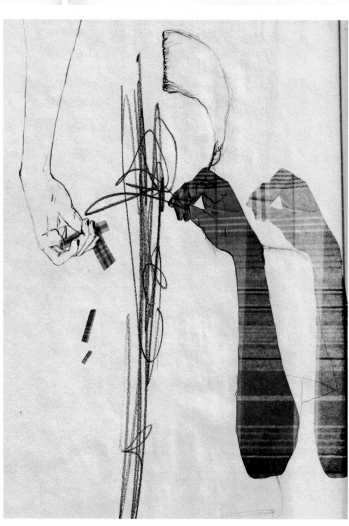

Sabine Pieper

Title: Anything (But)
(top)
Technique: Mixed media
2009

Untitled
(bottom left)
Technique: Mixed media
2009

Untitled
(bottom right)
Technique: Mixed media
2009

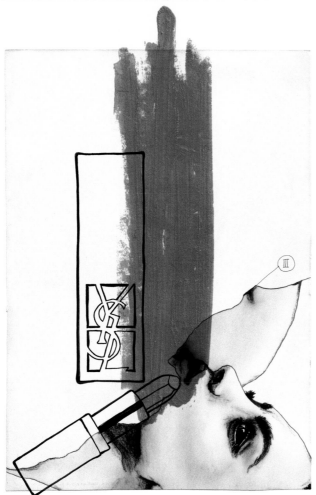

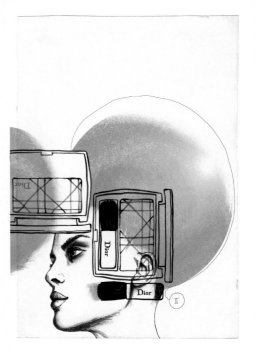

Gisela Goppel

All Images
Technique
Ink, watercolour, collage
2008

AMM
OU
UR

Gisela Goppel

All Images:
Technique:
ink, watercolour, collage
2008

Toril Bækmark

Title: Balldress
(top
Technique: Hand-drawn
ink, gouache
2009

Erin Petson

Title: Lanvin
(top right
Client
ST Magazine, The Telegraph
Format: Editorial
Technique
Pencil, ink, acrylic paint, collage
2009

Title: Vuitton
(bottom left
Client
ST Magazine, The Telegraph
Format: Editorial
Technique: Pencil, ink, paint
collage, Photoshop
2009

Title: Elephant Girl
(bottom right
Format: T-shirt
Technique: Pencil, ink, paint
collage, Photoshop
2009

Toril Bækmark

Title: Balldress
(top right)
Technique: Hand-drawn,
ink, gouache
2009

Annabel Briens

Untitled
(top left)
Client: Paris Match
Format: Editorial
Technique: Mixed media
2009

(bottom)
Client: Absolute Magazine
Format: Editorial
Technique: Mixed media
2007

Marguerite Sauvage

Title: Dolce Vita
(top)
Client: Virginie
Technique: Hand-drawn, digital
2008

Title: Jellyfishes
(right centre)
Client: Virginie
Technique: Hand-drawn, digital
2008

Title: Mellow Dream
(left centre)
Client: Grafuck Book
Format: Collective book
Technique: Hand-drawn, digital
2008

Title: Summer Ice Cream
(bottom)
Client: Grafuck Book
Format: Collective book
Technique: Hand-drawn, digital
2008

an Feindt

lient: Rosenthal
rt Director: Kirsten Voss
ormat: Coffee mug
echnique: Pen, brush, ink,
hotoshop
008

Marguerite Sauvag

Title: Fres
(top lef
Client: Und
Format: Variou
Technique: Pencil, digita
200

Title: Dress and Hai
(top righ
Client: Power in Number
Exhibition / Nucleu
Technique: Pencil, digita
200

Title: Parfur
(bottom lef
Clien
Ubisoft / Neko Entertainmen
Format: Video gam
Technique: Pencil, digita
200

Title: Dress and Hai
(bottom right
Client: Power in Number
Exhibition / Nucleu
Technique: Pencil, digita
200

Chico Hayasaki

Untitled
(top left)
Client: Elle e Seoul magazine
Format: Cover illustration
Technique:
Watercolour, ink, digital
2008

Untitled
(top right)
Technique:
Watercolour, ink, digital
2008

Title: Anemone
(bottom left)
Client: Anan magazine,
Magazine House
Format: Editorial
Technique:
Watercolour, ink, digital
2007

Title: Glimmer of Autumn
(bottom right)
Client: Four Seasons magazine,
Pace Communications
Art Director: Jaimey Easler
Format: Editorial
Technique:
Watercolour, ink, digital
2008

Bella Pilar

Title: Couture Girls Series
Format: Limited edition prints
Technique: Gouache
2008

Loreto Binvignat Streeter

Title: Cowgirrrl
(top left)
Client: Maomao Publications
Format: Book illustration
Technique: Pencil, watercolour
2008

Title: Bear Bear Furrr
(top right)
Client: Maomao Publications
Format: Book illustration
Technique: Pencil, watercolour
2008

Ana Laura Perez

Title: Girl
(bottom left)
Technique: Pencil, watercolour
2009

Untitled
(bottom right)
Technique: Pencil, watercolour
2009

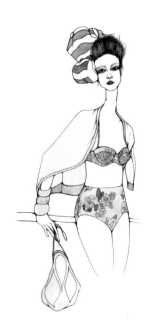

Anne Lück

Title: Bird
(top)
Client: Encore Magazine
Art Buyer: Patrick M. Sommer
Art Director: Daniel Harrington
Format: Cover illustration
Technique
Hand-drawn, Photoshop
2007

Title: Candida Albicans
(bottom left)
Client: Jungsheft
Art Director: Amélie Schneider
Format: Editorial
Technique
Hand-drawn, Photoshop
2007

Title: My Deer
(bottom upper right)
Client: 3 x 3 Ill09
Credits: Publisher & Design
Director: Charles Hively
Format: Editorial
Technique:
Hand-drawn, Photoshop
2009

Title: Tinte
(bottom lower right)
Technique:
Hand-drawn, Photoshop, collage
2008

Anne Lück

Title: The Two of Us
(top)
Technique:
Hand-drawn, Photoshop
2009

Title: Diary2
(bottom upper left)
Client: 3 x 3 Magazine
Credits: Publisher & Design
Director: Charles Hively
Format: Editorial
Technique:
Hand-drawn, Photoshop, collage
2008

Title: Different Types of
Fragrance
(bottom lower left)
Client: Saisonelle
Art Buyer: Lars Willumeit &
Helen van Pernis
Format: Editorial
Technique:
Hand-drawn, Photoshop
2008

Title: Louiza
(bottom right)
Hand-drawn, Photoshop
2008

Vincent Bakkum

Title: Altina
(top left)
Technique: Acrylic on canvas
2008

Title: Teen Joy
(top right)
Technique: Acrylic on canvas
2009

Title:
Bevrediging der Geslachtsdrift
(bottom left)
Technique: Acrylic on canvas
2009

Title: Chloé
(bottom right)
Client: Barcelona Mag
Format: Editorial
Technique: Acrylic on canvas
2008

Vincent Bakkum

Title: Red Birds and Plums
(top upper left)
Technique: Acrylic on canvas
2008

Title: Green Birds and Pears
(top lower left)
Technique: Acrylic on canvas
2008

Title: Ophéli
(top right)
Technique: Acrylic on canvas
2008

Title: Recipe Girl
(bottom left)
Technique: Acrylic on canvas
2007

Title: Delpnine
(bottom right)
Technique: Acrylic on canvas
2008

Vincent Bakkum
Title: Fere girl
Client: Menswear boutique Fere
Technique: Acrylic on canvas
2006

Vincent Bakkum

Title: Girl With White Gloves
(top)
Technique: Acrylic on canvas
2009

Title: Fere Girls
(bottom)
Client: Menswear boutique Fere
Technique: Acrylic on canvas
2007

Na

Title: Han
(top left
Technique
Hand-drawn, Photoshop
2006

Title: Let Us Lay in the Pink Peta
(top right
Technique
Hand-drawn, Photoshop
2009

Title
Frida Hyvonen / Silence is Wild
(bottom
Client: Plan B magazine
Format: Editorial
Technique
Hand-drawn, Photoshop
2008

Let us lay in the pink petal

Nao

Untitled
(top left)
Technique:
Hand-drawn, Photoshop
2009

Title: I Don't Care
(top right)
Technique:
Hand-drawn, Photoshop
2009

Title: Scenic World
(bottom)
Technique:
Hand-drawn, Photoshop
2009

Vicki Fong

Title: Rituals –
The Black, Gold & Red Series
All images
Technique
Hand-drawn, Photoshop
2009

Leslie Clerc

Title: Magazine Cover and Poster
(top)
Client: Dreams Magazine
Technique: Ink, Photoshop
2008

Naja Conrad-Hansen

Title: Golden
(bottom left)
Technique: Ink
2008

Title: Rock me Amadeus 1
(bottom right)
Client: Grafuck
Technique:
Ink, pencil, Photoshop
2006

Susanne Deeker

Title: The Mask O:
The Red Death
(top left, bottom right,
Format: Book illustrations
Technique: Mixed
2008

Untitled
(top right, top lower right, bottom left,
Client: Marc Jacob:
Technique: Mixed
2008

Naja Conrad-Hansen

Title: Hej
(top left)
Technique: Oil on linen
2008

Title: Hypnotising Chickens
(top right)
Technique: Oil on linen
2008

Title: F2
(bottom left)
Format: Editorial
Technique: Ink, Photoshop
2007

Title: Monkey On My Back
(bottom right)
Technique: Ink
2006

David Bra

Title: Even if I Fly I Still Love Yo
(Shallow? Deep
(top lef
Technique: Pen, pencil on pape
200

Title: By Night + By Da
(top upper right — 2 image
Client: Eyestor
Format: Limited print editio
Techniqu
Pen, pencil, paint on pape
200

Title: Bad Wisdom
(top lower righ
Client: Attention Spam grou
show, Schoeni Gallery Hong Kon
Technique: Pen, pencil on pape
2006

Title: I Never Saw the Sig
(bottom
Client: Code magazin
Format: Editoria
Technique: Pen, pencil, marke
200

Makiko Sugawa

Title: Break an Egg
(top upper left)
Client: Space Yui
Format: Exhibition show
Technique: Drawing, paint
2008

Title: Maria and Mari
(top centre)
Client: Compound gallery
Format: Exhibition show
Technique: Drawing, paint
2008

Title: Knitting
(top left bottom)
Client: Space Yui
Format: Exhibition show
Technique: Drawing, paint
2007

Title: Dolls
(top right)
Client: Space Yui
Format: exhibition show
Technique: Drawing
2009

Title: Android
(bottom)
Client: Syueisha
Credits: Subaru
Format: Illustration of a poem
Technique: Drawing
2007

Ink & Pencil

All ideas have a point of origin: they ferment and emerge from our minds, half-baked or fully-formed, in a wide variety of manifestations. A word, a sentence, a giggle, a scribble: most of these do not even make it past our internal control mechanism, our own harshest critic, and never see the light of day.

A pity, really, because in their undiluted and unfiltered state, these outbursts of unconscious spontaneity, of uncensored flows from mind to hand, yield plenty of diamonds in the rough, crusty gems that shine all the more for their makeshift nature.

Akin to the mindless scribbles and sketches dashed out on the notepad during a call, the power of association and associative evolution serves as springboard for creation and can lead to artworks of stunning intricacy.

Starting from a central scribble or key motif, a silly mistake or pretty pattern, the following works conquer the page in a gradual, open evolution. Unfettered by pre-determination, each stroke opens up a new possibility, a new path to be explored. Following the seams and ramifications, the pen rules the pencileer, the pattern the subject, until it loses its focus towards the edges for a hint of more to come.

In their raw immediacy, these works are rarely finished or defined. Instead, they claim the place and space they inhabit, state their character and individuality like graffiti on a page. Here, blobs and splotches serve as aesthetic Rorschach tests, as starting points for the emergence of new potential. Caught up in the thrall of creation, illustrators pick the nearest tool—ink, pencil, ballpoint pen, marker, watercolour—and when there is no paper in reach, pretty much any surface will do: skin, pianos, walls or old ledgers. Yet despite their delicious immediacy, the final results betray prodigious skill. Just like ideas, talent seeks its creative outlet!

Among the artists depicted here, some indulge in the almost autistic pleasure of repetition that they refine with each monotonous iteration. In their organic sprawls of tiny elements—one of them showing the "father of evolution", Charles Darwin, himself—the simple building blocks of life retrace the origins of creation. With each minute change and mutation they slowly evolve into entire bodies, filled with flowers and wildlife, to yield parallel strains and ecosystems, united in one illustration. In this, we witness the evolution of both creativity and skill—within the scope of a single page.

Arnika Müll

Untitled
Format: Exhibition
Technique: Fineliner on paper
2008

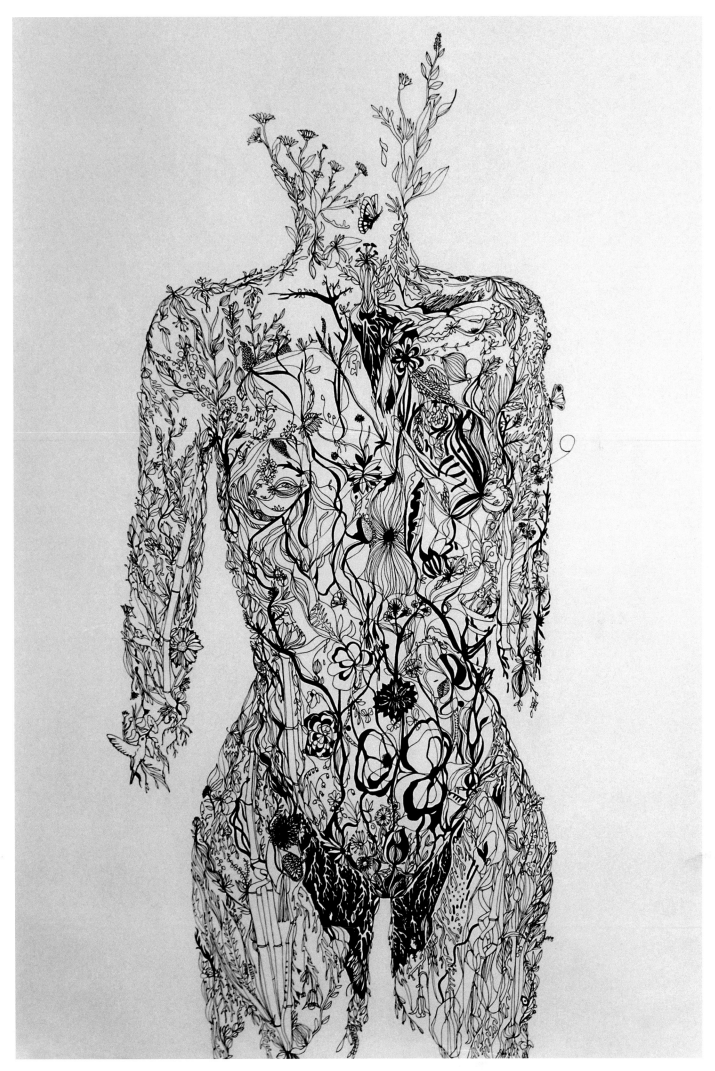

Jun Kaneko

Title: Lost
(top left and right, bottom right)

Title: Flower
(bottom left)

Technique: Acrylic on canvas
2009

Toril Bækmark

Title: Opium
Technique: Hand-drawn, ink,
Indian ink and Photoshop
2009

Toril Bækmar

Title: Ede
Technique: Hand-drawn
ink, Indian ink and Photosho
2009

Daniel Egnéus

Title: Hengirl
(top left)
Technique: Ink, pencil
2009

Title: Sharkgirl
(top right)
Technique: Ink
2009

Title: Balletgirl
(bottom left)
Technique: Ink, pencil
2009

Title: Polar Bear Girl
(bottom right)
Technique: Watercolour, pencil
2009

Lapin

Title: Expediciones de Lapin
(top, middle)
Format: Self-published art book
Technique: Hand-drawn,
watercolour, ink pen
2008

Title: Home Alone
(bottom)
Client: L'appart PR
Format: Editorial
Technique: Hand-drawn,
watercolour, ink pen, Photoshop
2008

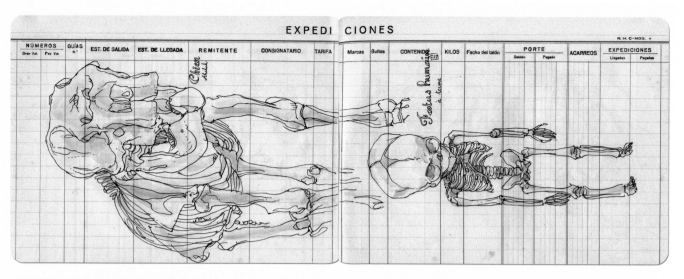

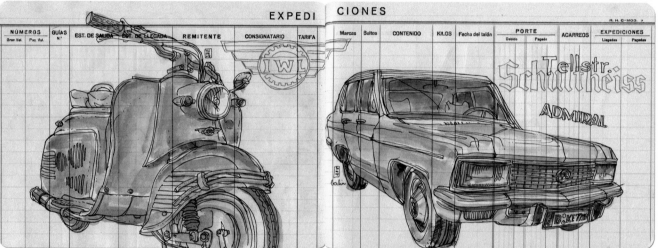

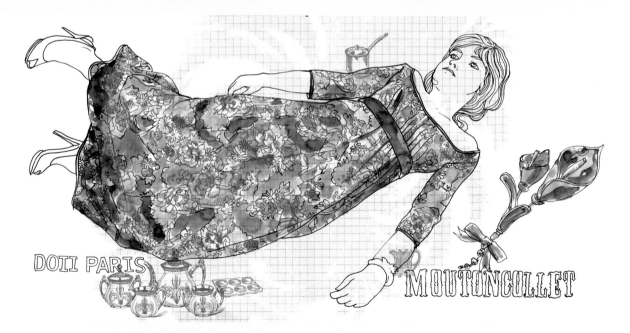

Lapin

Title: Expediciones de Lapin
(top, middle)
Format: Self-published art book
Technique: Hand-drawn,
watercolour, ink pen
2008

Title: Seat 600
(bottom left)
Technique: Hand-drawn,
watercolour, ink pen
2009

Title: Very Latest Style
(bottom right)
Technique: Hand-drawn,
watercolour, ink pen

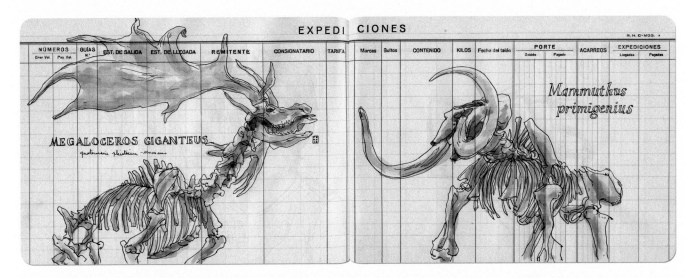

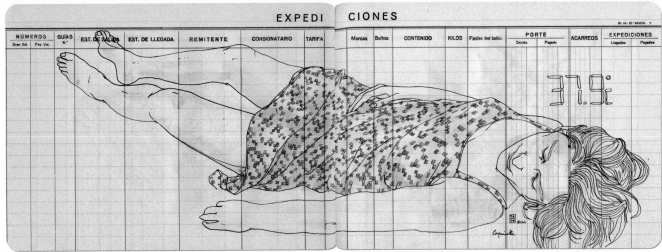

Interview Gabriel Moreno

Self-confessed "creative, stubborn, passionate, demanding nutcase" Gabriel Moreno thrives on the natural evolution of thoughts and ideas. Unfurling across his chosen canvas—page, façade or even skin—his tattoo-like creations spin their own stories from a filigree web of Pilot pen lines.

Background

Ever since I was a kid, I have been attracted to lines and light. I guess I was your average boy who spent hours in front of the box, watching cartoons, drawings, comics or movies. Once I got hold of a pencil, there simply was no stopping me. In school I always got into trouble for drawing on the tables!
I ended up studying Fine Arts in Seville and later moved to Madrid. Ever since I finished my portfolio, I have pretty much lived with it tucked under my arm, working non-stop for agencies, magazines and others who allow me to combine the "commercial" aspect with my passion for painting.

Skills and Techniques

There are many people I admire, e. g. Berto Martínez, Alex Trouchut, Serial Cut or Eva Solano, but my biggest passion and inspiration remains beauty in all its shapes and guises; all those little things that shake me up and inject me with the necessary energy to think, feel and do what I do.
In a way, I draw what beauty makes me "feel"—illustration gives me the opportunity to make it mine somehow and give it a new form and outlet.
I might start from a very simple premise—say, a gesture, the shape of a mouth, a chance encounter on the street or the movement of my wife crossing her legs—but then my lines start to tangle, intersect and mix, giving rise to a new figure, then another one ... a man, a woman, a bird, a bird-man.

Inspiration and Influences

Despite my studies, I am mainly self-taught. Illustration gives me the chance to work in a huge variety of different fields and genres. For example, I really enjoy working on my personal and more traditional projects as a painter and engraver. For my illustrations, I use pens, pencils, crayons, watercolours ... whatever is at hand. Although most of them are done with a Pilot pen, I do love working with new materials. Most of my works combine traditional techniques with new technologies and I could not do without this mix.

Featured Works

Creation is my life and that is why it is so easy for me to pour my heart and art into it. And who would have thought that I might grace an LA Times cover or that my illustration would cover one of the most famous buildings of Madrid's Gran Vía?

Gabriel Moreno

Title: Head
Technique: Pen
2007

En Repsol hemos producido en un año
más de 500 km de asfalto a partir de neumáticos desechados.
Una iniciativa que contribuye a reducir el impacto medioambiental,
el impacto acústico y mejora la seguridad vial.

Inventemos el futuro

Gabriel Moreno

Title: Mano
(top left
Client: Repsol YPF
Agency: Young & Rubicam
Format: Advertising
Technique
Pencil, colour pen
2008

Title: Pierna
(top right
Client: Repsol YPF
Agency: Young & Rubicam
Format: Advertising
Technique
Pencil, colour pen
2008

Title: Marlboro
(bottom
Client: Marlboro
Agency: La DesPens
Format: Video
Technique: Pencil and pen
2008

*¿Cómo no vamos a ser capaces de inventar
el camino de vuelta a casa?*

En Repsol hemos desarrollado una nueva generación de plásticos para invernaderos
que permiten disfrutar de cultivos diversificados y
respetuosos con el medio ambiente en cualquier época del año
Inventemos el futuro

*¿Cómo no vamos a ser capaces de hacer
que sea siempre primavera?*

Gabriel Moreno

Title:
Pájaro, Mariposa, Pavo Real
(3 images clockwise from top)
Format: Exhibition
Technique:
Pilot pen, watercolour
2009

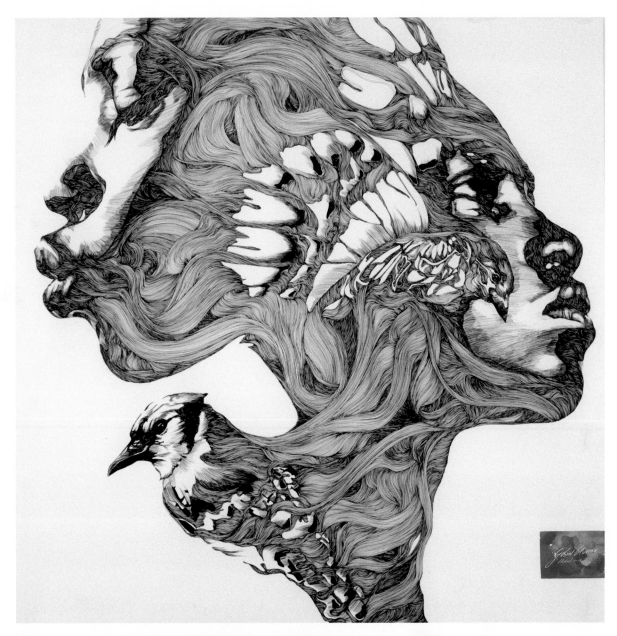

Hjärta Smärta

Title: Mont Blanc
Client: Pen Magazine
Format: Editorial
Technique: Collage
2008

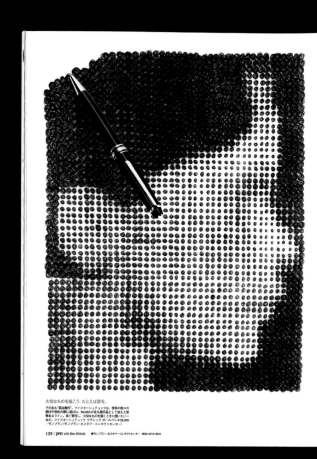

Sophie Henson

Title: Connections
(top)
Technique: Hand-drawn,
Illustrator, Photoshop
2009

Billie Jean

Title:
Samaritans "Doodle" Campaign
(centre, bottom)
Client: Samaritans
Agency: Lunar BBDO
Format: Advertising
Technique:
Hand-drawn, Photoshop.
2006

Otto Björni

Title: A Cut Above the Res
(top lef

Title: D
(top righ

Title: Ma Bella Lun
(bottom lef

Title: Alekhine's Defenc
(bottom righ

All image
Format: Commissione
Technique: Pen, in
2008/

Sarah King

Title: Up In The Flies
(top left)

Title: Charles Darwin
(top right)

Title:
Thomas "Blackjack" Ketchum
(bottom left)

Title: Jaques Cousteau
(bottom right)

ll images:
Technique: Drawing
2009

Ana Bagayan

Title: Chelsea
(top left)
Technique: Pencil on paper
200

Title: Harriet
(top right)
Technique: Pencil on paper
200

Title: Franci
(bottom left)
Technique: Pencil on paper
200

Title: Claire
(bottom right)
Technique: Pencil on paper
2008

CHELSEA upon waking, was displeased to discover that the bed bugs she had so faithfully fed were now feeding on her lower half.

HARRIET is stuck with the unfortunate burden of having large eyes and practicing as a peeping tom.

FRANCIE feared removing her amulet, not out of superstition, but to hide her mysterious tuft of stray hairs.

CLAIRE has decided to coat her one true love in glue to peel off a perfect replica should he expire.

Hiroshi Tanabe

Title: Alexander McQueen
(top left)
Client: Dune
Art Direction: Hideki Nakajima,
Fumihiro Hayashi
Format: Editorial
Technique: Pen, printing
1996

Untitled
(top right)
Client: Nico (Luxembourg)
Art Direction: Elisa Kern,
Guido Kroger
Format: Editorial
Technique: Pen, pencil,
Photoshop
2008

Untitled
(bottom left)
Client: United Bamboo
Art Direction: Nobutaka Kaneko
Format: T-shirt
Technique: Pen, Photoshop
2007

Title: Marie Antoinette
(bottom right)
Client: Art Days Publishing
Art Director: Fumihiro Hyashi
Format: Movie catalogue / Dune
Technique: Pen, Photoshop
2007

Dan Abbot

Title: Face Fog
(top)
Technique: Ink on paper
2009

Title: Wind Phoenix
(bottom left)
Technique: Ink on paper
2009

Pandarosa

Title: Time is Money
(bottom right)
Client
Galerie Heliumcowboy Artspace
Format: Artwork
Technique: Pen on paper
2008

Jesus L. Yapor

Title: Couple
(top left)
Technique: Pen on paper
2007

Title: The Fortune Teller
(middle left)
Technique: Pen on paper
2007

Title: Geometric Fairy
(middle centre)
Technique: Pen on paper
2007

Title: Supplicating
(middle right)
Technique: Pen on paper
2007

Sopp Collective

Title: FBi sounds
(top right)
Artist: Katja Hartung
Client: FBi radio
Format: Web
Technique: Felt tip, digital collage
2008

Marianna Rossi

Title: De Rerum Natura
(bottom — 2 images)
Technique: Black ink on paper
2007

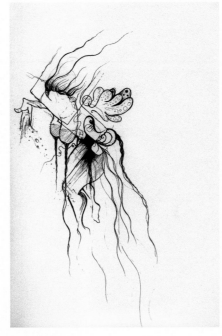

Steffi Lindner

Title: Der Einzelne I / II / III
Client: Exhibition work
    for Bipolar
Technique: Mixed media on wood
    2007

Steffi Lindner

Title: Sylvia P.
(top left)
Client: Exhibition work
for Blütenweiss
Technique:
Acrylic, pencil on paper
2008

Title: Gier
(top right)
Client: Exhibition work
for Blütenweiss
Technique:
Acrylic, pencil on paper
2008

Title: Promise
(bottom left)
Client: Exhibition work
for Blütenweiss
Technique:
Acrylic, pencil on paper
2008

Title: Skinny legs
(bottom right)
Technique: Acrylic, pencil
on paper, Photoshop
2009

Evelyn Hahn

Title: Inszenierung der Mode
(top + bottom right)
Format: Exhibition piece
Technique: Etching
2008

Untitled
(bottom left)
Format: Exhibition piece
Technique: Mixed media on canvas
2008

Evelyn Hahn

Title: Black Haired Woman
(top)
Format: Exhibition piece
Technique: Mixed media on canvas
2008

Untitled
(bottom left)
Technique: Hand-drawn, collage
2008

Untitled
(bottom right)
Technique: Acrylic on wood
2008

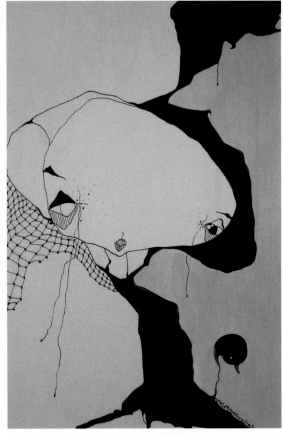

Sandrine Pagnou

Title: Pin U
(top lef

Title: I Can See You In The Chac
(top righ

Title: I Kill Myse
(bottom lef

Title: Ghost Danc
(bottom righ

All image
Technique: Drawin
2007/

Daniel Egnéus

Title: Rites of Spring 3
(top left)
Technique: Ink
2009

Title: Pierrot
(bottom)
Client: La Perla
Technique: Watercolour
2008

Stina Persson

Title: Cheek
(top right)
Format: For the "La Femme" show
at Gallery Nucleus, Alhambra
Technique: Indian ink, paper
2008

2 Spécimen n°483438-r
Cat : monster mind type2
Capture 05.12.86 -01h13mn

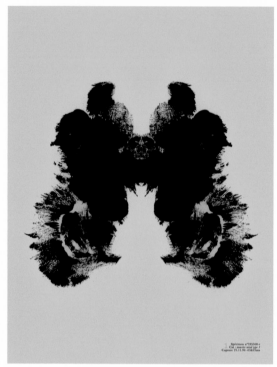

1 Spécimen n°593508-r
Cat : monster mind type 1
Capture 25.11.86 -01h53mn

Stéphane Goddar

Title: Mind Monster
(top left and right
Format: Exhibition
Technique: Painting, digita
2008

Woo

Title: Headz 02 + 04
(bottom left, bottom lower right
Format: Poster
Technique: Photoshop
2008

Title: WKT Goo
(bottom upper right
Client: Wieden + Kennedy Tokyo
Art Director: +Cru
Format: Mura
Technique: Illustrator
2008

Pandarosa

Title: Nocturnal Spring
(top left)
Client: Galerie Heliumcowboy
Format: Exhibition
Technique: Vinyl work on paper
2008

Title: Somewhere Between
Sunset and Sunrise
(top right)
Client: California State
University, Fullerton—
College of the Arts
Technique: Pen on paper
2009

Title: Time is Atrophy
(bottom left)
Client: Galerie Heliumcowboy
Format: Exhibition
Technique: Vinyl work on paper
2008

Title: She Tangled Her Hair
in the Clouds
(bottom right)
Client: California State
University, Fullerton—
College of the Arts
Technique: Pen on paper
2009

Alexander Ovchinnikov

Untitled
(all 3 images,
Technique: Digital
2008/9

Raquel Aparicio

Title: Horse
Client: Festival de El Sol
Format: Editorial
Technique: Hand-drawn
2009

Silja Goe

Title: Cup of Te
(top lef

Vin
(bottom lef

Pierna
(bottom righ

Format: Editoria
Technique
Brush, ink, watercolou
200

Leslie Cler

Title: Canal Themis Logo
(top righ
Client: French Ministry o
Justice's podcast and onlin
communication
Format: We
Technique: Photoshop, ink
200

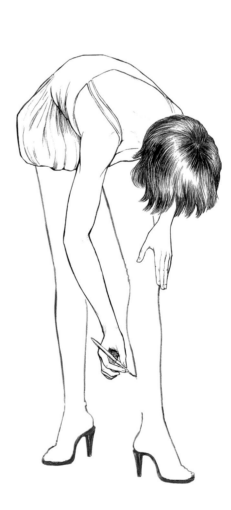

Raquel Aparicio

Title: Animals
(top left)
Client: Viajar Magazine
Art Director: Luís Uribarri
Format: Editorial
Technique: Ink drawing
2009

Title: Uzumaki Girl
(top right)
Client: Monster thread
Credits: Mark Mamot
Format: T-shirt
Technique: Ink
2009

Title: Candy
(bottom right)
Client: Lados Magazine
Art Director: Hanko Jacobsen
Format: Editorial
Technique: Ink
2008

Title: Literary Hotels
(bottom left)
Client: Viajar Magazine
Art Director: Antonio Arés
Format: Editorial
Technique: Ink
2008

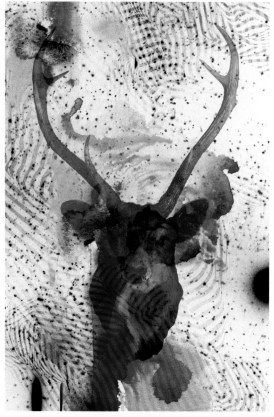

Tetsuya Toshima

Untitled
(top left)
Technique: Drawing, digital
2007

Untitled
(top right)
Client: iPhone / iPod
Touch / opps!
Technique:
Pencil, watercolour, digital
2009

Jules Julien

Title: Cadavres Exquis
(bottom left + right)
Client: Diesel Denim Gallery
Aoyama — Tokyo
Format: Limited edition
Technique: Digital drawing
2009

Tetsuya Toshima

Untitled
(top left + right)
Technique: Drawing, digital
2008/9

Jules Julien

Title: Cadavres Exquis
(bottom left + right)
Client: Diesel Denim Gallery
Aoyama—Tokyo
Format: Limited edition
Technique: Digital drawing
2009

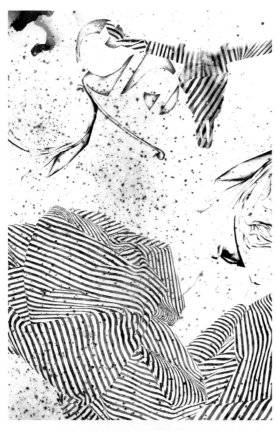

Hiroshi Tanabe

Untitled
(top upper left, top right)
Client: Graphic-sha Publishing
Art Director: Hideki Nakajima
Format: From my book called "#2"
Technique: Pen
2003

Untitled
(top lower left)
Client: GAP (USA)
Art Director: Carl Wolentarski
Format: T-shirt
Technique: Pen, Photoshop
2009

Stina Fisch

Untitled
(bottom, 3 images)
Title: Tijd (series)
Credits: Mike Koedinger éditions
Technique: Ink on paper
2008

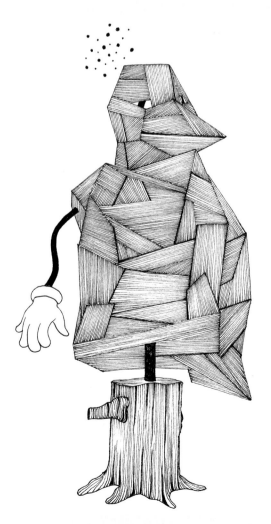

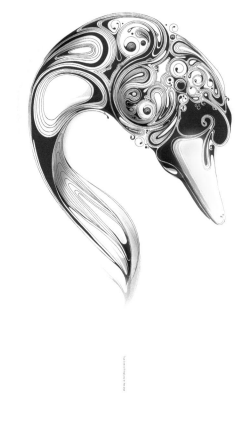

SiScott

Title: 21st Century Bible
(top left)
Client: Hodder & Stoughton
Format: Publishing
Technique: Hand-drawn
2008

Titles:
True Love Will Find You In
The End
(top right)
Client: Varsko 04
Format: Exhibition
Technique: Hand-drawn
2008

Title: Resonate / Stag
(bottom left)
Client: Silent Studios
Format: Packaging, print
Technique: Hand-drawn,
Photoshop
2008

Title: Havana
(bottom right)
Client: Havana
Photography &
Model Making: Si Scott
Format: Exhibition
Technique:
Hand-drawn, photo
2008

Dopludo

Title: Hairdrops
(top left)
Title: Eternal Inside
(top right)
Title: Lightbulb
(bottom left)
Eika, Dopludo collective
(bottom right)

all images:
Designer: Eika
Technique: Pencil
2008/9

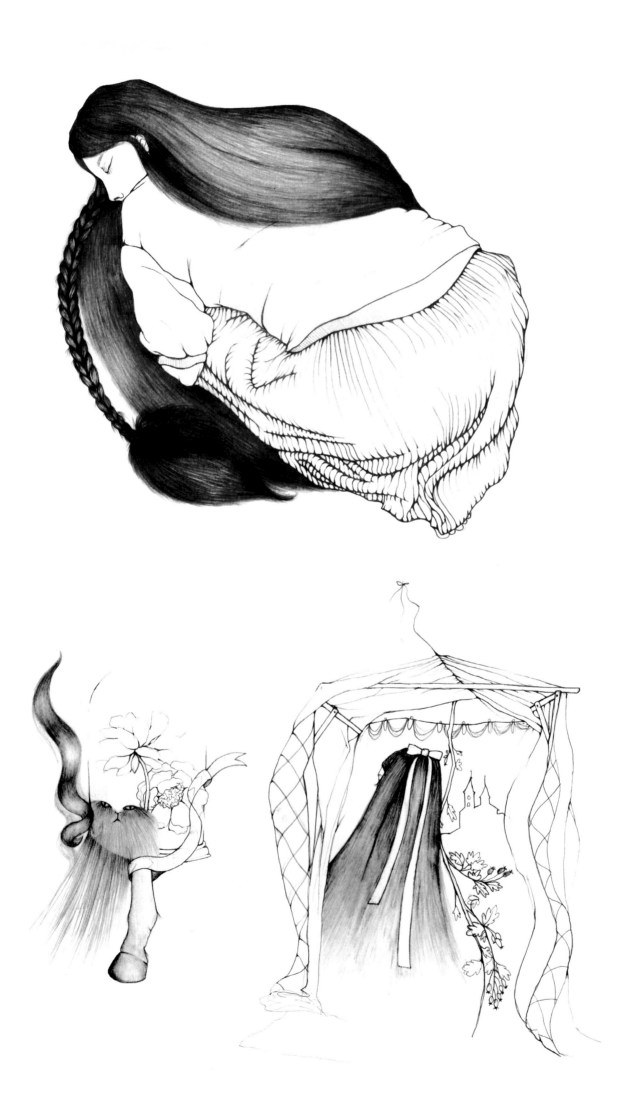

Ana Laura Perez

Title: Asleep
(top)
Technique: Pencil
2008

Title: Collage
(bottom)
Technique: Pencil
2007

Tanja Székessy

Title: Landleben
(top)
Technique: Pencil, Photoshop
2009

Title: Soupirs
(bottom)
Client: Slanted magazine #6
Art Director: Raban Ruddigkeit
Format: Editorial
Technique: Pencil, Photoshop
2009

Charlotte Delarue

Title: Rio
(top)
Client: Surface to Air
Format: T-shirt
Technique: Graphite
2008

Title: My Old Piano
(bottom right)
Client: Surface to Air
Format: T-shirt
Technique: Graphite
2008

Title: Lapis Lapin
(bottom left)
Format: Lapis Lapin exhibition
at Surface to Air in Sao Paulo
Technique:
Graphite, black ink
2008

Charlotte Delarue

Title: No Future
(top)
Client: Surface to Air
Technique: Graphite
2008

Title: Captain
(bottom left)
Client: Surface to Air
Technique: Graphite
2008

Title: Mechanics
(bottom right)
Client: Surface to Air
Format: T-shirt
Technique: Graphite
2008

Vania Zouravlio•

Title: Cherry Kal•
(top left•
Technique: Ink on paper
2009

Title: Dirty Little Finger•
(top right•
Technique: Ink on paper•
2008

Magnus Blomste•

Title: Untitled I•
(bottom left•
Technique: Hand-drawn•
2009

Title: Falling Dow•
(bottom upper right•
Technique•
Hand-drawn, Illustrato•
2008

Title: MMVIII—•
(bottom lower right•
Technique•
Hand-drawn, Illustrato•
2008

Vania Zouravliov

Title: Columbina
(top left)
Client: Diaghilev project
Technique: Ink on paper
2009

Title: Sleep of Jiang Shi
(top right)
Technique: Ink on paper
2009

Title: The Knife
(bottom left)
Client: Yaso magazine, Japan
Technique: Ink on paper
2008

Title: Ultrablack
(bottom right)
Client: Ici d'ailleurs, France
Format: Record sleeve for Matt
Elliott's "Howling Songs"
Technique: Ink on paper
2008

N8 Van Dyke

Title: A.D.
(top)

Title: She Will Die Like You And
(bottom left)

Title: Vic is Dead
(bottom right)

All images
Technique: Ink on paper
200

Valence

Title: Hazy
(top)
Technique: Mixed media
2008

Title: Hidden
(bottom left)
Client: Army of Art
Technique: Hand-drawn,
Photoshop
2009

Title: Distress
(bottom right)
Format: Exhibition piece
Technique: Hand-drawn,
Photoshop
2008

Samuel Casal

Title: Zeitgeist
Technique: Vectorial
2008

Title: Cordel From Hell
Le Voyeur
(top right, 2 images)
Client: Carranca
Format: T-shirt
Technique: Vectorial
2008

Title: Efeito Borboleta
(top lower right)
Client: It's Gallery
Format: T-shirt
Technique: Vectorial
2008

Stina Fisch

Title: Running backwards (series)
(bottom, 3 images)
Format: Solo show at CAPe
Luxembourg
Technique: Ink on cardboard
2009

Shohei

Title: Flight Girl
(top left)
Technique: Ballpoint pen, marker
2006

Title: Sayoko's Anger
(top right)
Technique: Ballpoint pen, marker
2008

Title: Motorcycle of Penis
(bottom left)
Technique: Ballpoint pen, marker
2006

Title: Cemetery of Jingi
(bottom upper right)
Technique: Ballpoint pen, marker
2004

Title: Akane's Death
(bottom lower right)
Technique: Ballpoint pen, marker
2009

Felix Gephar

Title: At Se
(top
Technique: Spray paint on wa
200

Untitle
(bottom left + right
Technique: Ink on pape
200

Silja Goetz

Title: Crisis
(top)
Art Director: Andreas Gnass
Format: Personal piece for Revue
Technique: Brush, ink
2009

Felix Gephart

Untitled
(bottom left + right)
Technique: Ink on paper
2008

Billie Jean

Title: Jack McManus Piano
All images
Client: Polydor Records
Universal Music
Art Director: Root Design
Format: Bespoke piano
for video Jack McManus
"Bang on the Piano"
Technique: Drawn, painted
2008

Lotie

Untitled
All images:
Client: Bloom magazine /
Edelkoort editions
Format: Editorial
Technique: Hand-drawn,
Photoshop
2008

Colin Henderson

Title: Black Marketto Black
Client: MISC-Magazine
Credits:
Format: A2 Poster
Technique: Hand-drawn
2008

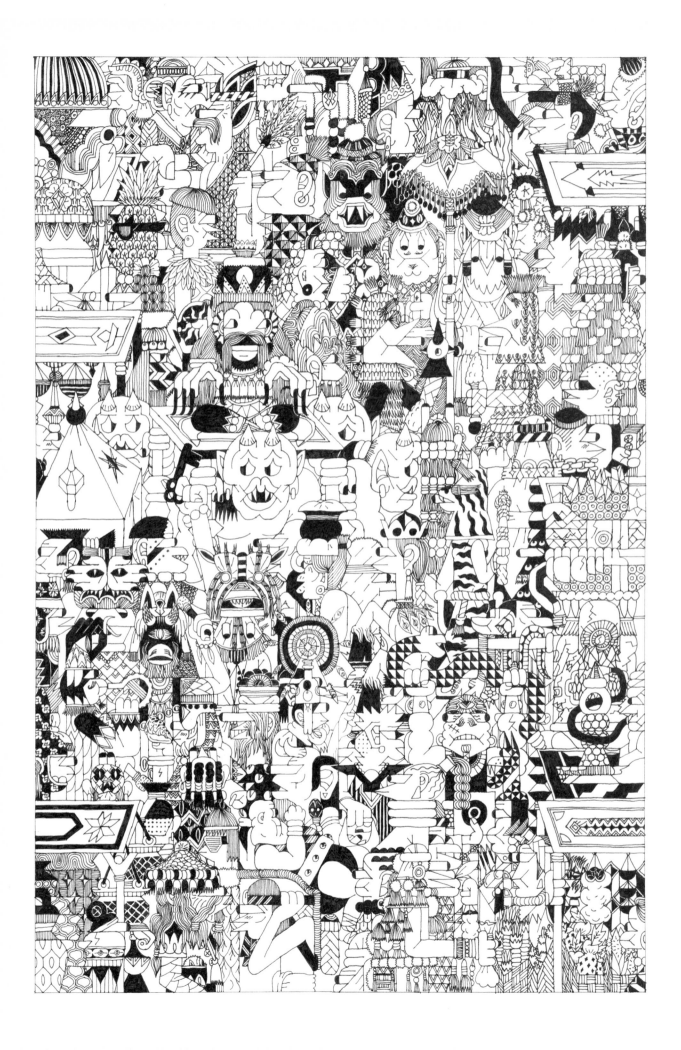

an Håkon Robson

Title: Loaf
Client: Loaf
Format: T-shirt
Technique: Hand-drawn
2008

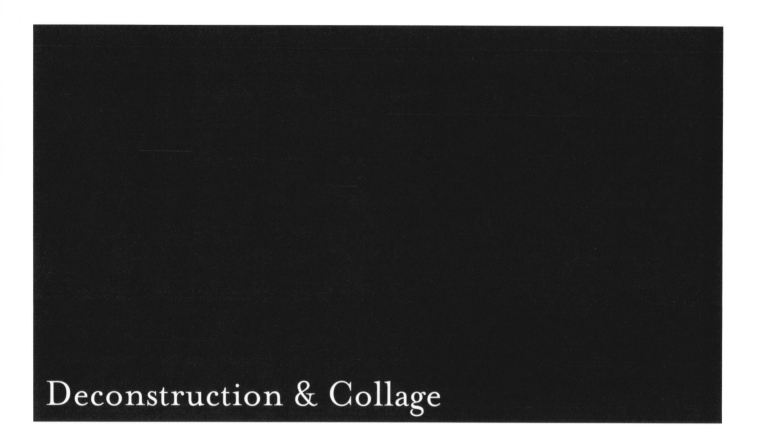

Deconstruction & Collage

Juxtaposition is a powerful tool—it can enhance, exaggerate, alienate, highlight, transpose, elevate and enrich: ripped out of its familiar surroundings, even nature becomes an alien force.

The cerebral stimulation of collage, its power to unsettle and liberate us, traces all the way back to our evolutionary roots—and the basic rules of expectation. Once something in our sight diverts from the norm, from our expected framework of visual references, it simultaneously disturbs and delights us. Take an infant's fascination with a ball that isn't there, with peek-a-boo and simple magic tricks—it simply does not compute with our preconceived notion. This constant, and unconscious, comparison to a baseline reality carries a vital evolutionary advantage: it allows us to learn and anticipate.

With age and experience the shock value lessens, and this is equally relevant to the genre of deconstruction itself. No longer the bad boy and wild child of the art world, collage needed its own subversive refresher course. In this chapter, the popular staple of broadsheet illustration tears away from the mid-brow context to re-explore its 20th century roots—Dada, Surrealism, Deconstructivism and underground culture.

Mixing media, techniques and technologies with wild abandon, our protagonists bend the world to their own rules, then recreate it from the rubble. In their lust for imperfection, for rough edges and aesthetic refusal, they slash the clean lines of cleaned-up designs, the smooth swoops of digital perfection, to play with sizes and angles, dimensions and characters, fabrics, textures and sentiments. Thus picked apart and reassembled, their brave new world is never quite right—and rightly so.

Snatched from time and aesthetic context, old school Deconstructivism and poster design meet classic 1990s MTV punk, found objects and knowingly contrite clip art; yet their creators' motivation is no longer punk per se, i. e. political opinion or lack of funds (think glue, photocopies and safety pins), but based on individual and individualised counterclaims to 20th century Constructivism and Futurism.

In their enforced entropy and deliberate disintegration of form, colour and content, they dip into the entire bell curve of deconstructive variants; from abstract, almost clinical assemblages to the viscerally grotesque. For reference, try the nip and tuck of Hans Bellmer's modern-day homunculi, cut-up bodies reassembled into man-machines, Kurt Schwitter's Dadaist "Psychological Collage", the disjointed machinations of Picabia or the methodical madness Dr. Bronner's Magic Soap, where words and icons disappear in an insanely condensed convolute of visual information.

Here, deconstruction and reassembly become a cipher for the illustrated message, hidden underneath broken layers of meaning. Once we decode the hidden key, however, it becomes all the more satisfying. A suggestive force, these images show us what isn't and—maybe—shouldn't be, but hint at the possibility.

Emmanuel Polanco

Title: The Fool
Credits: Ship of Fools exhibition
Format: Exhibition
Technique: Collage
2009

Emmanuel Polanco

Title: Edgar Allan Poe
USPS Commemorative
Edition book stamps
Client: US Postal Service
Credits: Colagene and Journey
Director: Mike Ryan
Format: Editorial
Technique: Collage
2009

Emmanuel Polanco

Title: Tigre et Corbeau
Technique: Collage
2009

LE TIGRE
ET OFFROY LE
CORBEAU

Mathilde Aubier

Title: Les Parents de Mélie
(top left)
Client: Les éditions Syros
Format: Book cover
Technique: Collage
2009

Title: Conseils à Éviter
(top right)
Client: Jeune et jolie
Format: Editorial
Technique: Collage
2009

Title: Kaléidoscope
(bottom left)
Format: Poster
Technique: Collage
2009

Title: Automne
(bottom upper right)
Client: Uzik
Format: Identity
Technique: Collage
2008

Title: Love dreams
(bottom lower right)
Client: Jeune et jolie
Format: Editorial
Technique: Collage
2009

Emmanuel Polanco

Title: Dad
(top right)
Client: Milk magazine
Technique: Collage
2009

Untitled
(left — 2 images)
Client: Katherine Mez
Format: Record sleeve
Technique: Collage
2008

Title:
Le Pendu — Tarot de Marseille
(bottom right)
Technique: Collage
2008

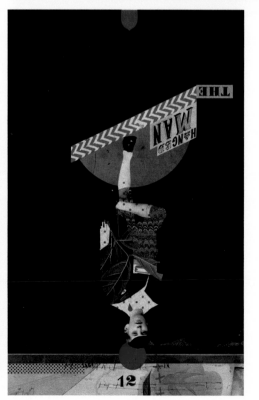

Eduardo Recife

Title: New Heights
(top left)
Technique: Digital collage
2008

Title: Map of the Interior World
(top right)
Technique: Digital collage
2008

Title: Truth
(bottom left)
Technique: Digital collage
2008

Title: Love
(bottom right)
Technique: Digital collage
2007

Maximo Tuja

Title: Aludd
Client: Dududá, Barcelona
Format: Exhibition
Technique: Collage,
Hand-drawn, Photoshop
2008

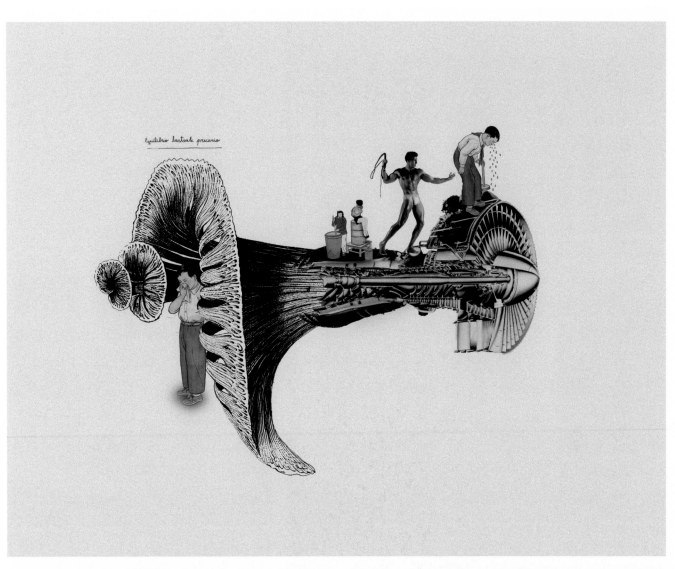

Handiedar

Title: Toile
(top left
Format: Exhibition
Technique: Mixed media
2009

Title: I Love Sno White No.
(top right
Format: Exhibition
Technique: Mixed media
2007

Title:
Who Said That We Need to be
Strong?
(bottom
Client: Fefé magazine
Credits: Luigi Vernier
Format: Editorial
Technique: Mixed media
2007

Handiedan

Title: Pin-up Tree No. 2
(top left)
Format: Exhibition
Technique: Mixed media
2007

Title: Popeye No. 2
(top right)
Format: Exhibition
Technique: Mixed media
2008

Title: Queen of Hearts No. 2
(bottom left)
Format: Exhibition
Technique: Mixed Media
2008

Title: I Do Models
(bottom right)
Client: Subtle Disruption
Credits: Nav Chatterji
Format: T-shirt
Technique: Mixed media
2008

Luca Schenardi

Title:
Das vermeintlich leichte Spiel
(top left)

Title: Die Ankunft
(top right)

Title: Wenn die Bank erwacht
(right centre)

Title: Geissbock
(bottom)

Client: Fumetto Festival —
D.I.J.D.S.D.
Format: Editorial
Technique: Mixed media
2009

Mone Maurer

Title:
Das Geheimnis des Fußballs
ist ja der Ball—Uwe Seeler
(left—3 images)
Client: Null Acht—
Zeitung für Fußball und Sport
Format: Editorial
Technique: Mixed media
2008

Title: This is Michael
(top right)
Client: +rosebud Magazine
Format: Editorial
Technique: Mixed media
2009

Title: Artwork for Diesel
Concept Store Berlin-Mitte
(bottom right)
Client: Diesel
Format: Paint on canvas
Technique: Mixed media
2009

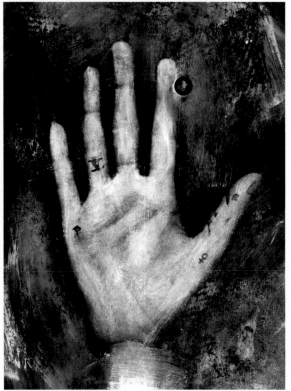

Jacob Arden McClure

Title: Nazi Muffin
(top left)
Client: Pretty Picture Movement
Format: Editorial
Technique: Photoshop
2008

Title: Flying
(top right)
Client: Applegate Gallery
Format: Exhibition
Technique: Photoshop
2007

Title: Running with Guns
(bottom left)
Client: Applegate Gallery
Format: Exhibition
Technique: Photoshop
2007

Title: Dive In
(bottom right)
Client: Applegate Gallery
Format: Exhibition
Technique: Photoshop
2007

Tara Hardy

Title: The Collection
(top left)
Client: The Globe and Mail
Format: Editorial
Technique: Collage
2009

Title: The Complete Artist
(top right)
Client:
Wax Communications—Honens
Format: Poster
Technique: Collage, mixed media
2009

Title: The Vodka Martini
(bottom)
Client: The Globe and Mail
Format: Editorial
Technique: Collage, mixed media
2009

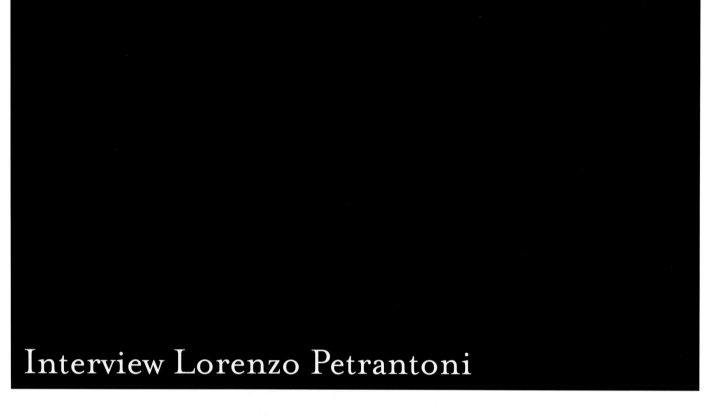

Interview Lorenzo Petrantoni

The devil is in the detail: dense, methodical and bristling with (visual) information, Lorenzo Petrantoni's Victorian clip art extravaganzas appropriate 19th century icons and tycoons, slogans and classifieds to reorder and reassess reality as we know it. Unlike other Deconstructivists, the Milan-based illustrator's work is not about destruction but rediscovery. Whipped into shape by the formal corset of stern geometry, his assemblages thrive on organised chaos and carefully controlled information overload, firmly anchored in its own past.

Background

I was born in Genoa on the 17th of October 1970. After attending advertising school in Milan, I worked as an art director for a number of agencies before focussing on illustration.

Skills and Techniques

I am entirely self-taught: I have no academic training, it is just a passion and craft I have acquired myself. Everything is done by hand. I hate computers!
For installations, I print the details of my illustrations on separate sheets and then stack them by hand. This adds a certain volume to my work and turns each installation into a distinct, unique project.

Inspiration and Influences

I love graphic art and old books. I want to bring them back to life, discover their stories and tell the present through the past. I draw most of my inspiration from late 19th century encyclopaedias—this particular period in time is very important to me. When I scour old tomes for suitable images, I give these books, events and characters a new lease on life and make sure they are not forgotten on the shelves of some dusty bookshop.
To me, black and white are truly timeless. If used well, they can be stronger than a full rainbow of colours.

Featured Works

While I prefer to work for publishing, as it allows the most leeway and freedom of expression, I also try my hand at other outlets, e. g. wine bottles, snowboards, apparel, etc. My personal favourite is an illustration called Bolas, a reproduction of all of the circles found in a dictionary from 1920.

Lorenzo Petrantoni

Title: Statua
Technique: Encyclopaedic collage
2007

Lorenzo Petrantoni

Title: Inf
(top)
Client: Diximedia Digital
Art Director: Quique Infante
Format: Editorial
Technique:
Encyclopaedic collage
2009

Title: Wired
(centre)
Client: Wired Magazine
Credits: Margaret
Format: Editorial
Technique:
Encyclopaedic collage
2009

Title: Sole
(bottom)
Client: Sole 24 ore Magazine
Art Director: Giuseppe Centrone
Format: Editorial
Technique:
Encyclopaedic collage
2009

Lorenzo Petrantoni

Title: Foundations
(top)
Client: The New York Times
Designer: Leo Jung
Format: Editorial
Technique:
Encyclopaedic collage
2008

Title: Modern
(bottom left)
Client: Sole 24 Ore Magazine
Art Director: Madda Paternoster
Format: Editorial
Technique:
Encyclopaedic collage
2008

Title: Dog
(bottom right)
Client: Los Angeles Time
Format: Editorial
Technique:
Encyclopaedic collage
2009

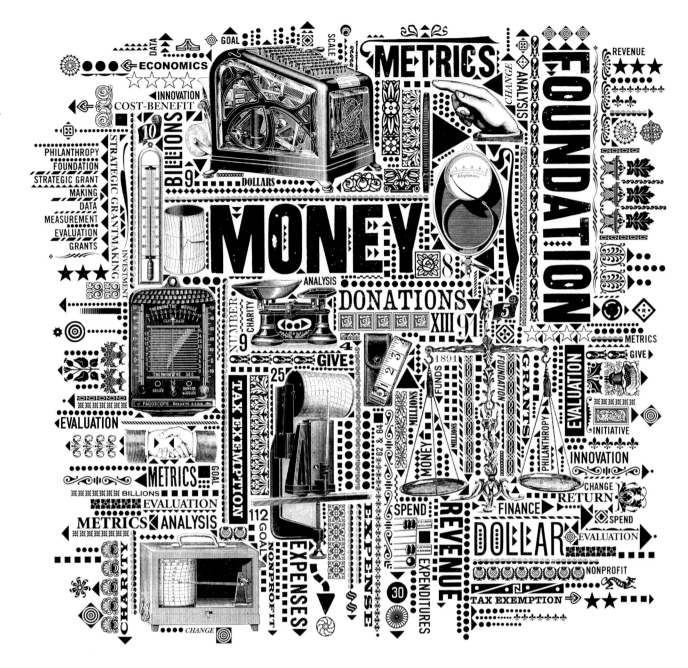

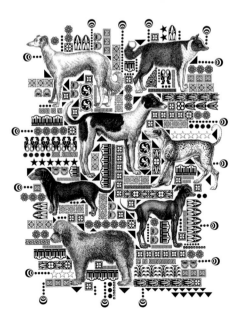

Skizzoma

Title: Work-life balance
(top)
Client: Emotion magazine
Format: Editorial
Technique: Analog-digital collage
2009

Title: 198
(bottom left)
Client: Destructed magazine
Format: Editorial
Technique: Analog-digital collage
2006

Title: Fashion Berlin–New York
(bottom right)
Client: Zitty magazin
Format: Editorial
Technique: Analog-digital collage
2008

Eva Eun-sil Han

Title: Spit-out
(top)

Title: Achluophobia
(bottom left)

Title: Noon
(bottom right)

All images:
Technique: Mixed media on paper
2008

Jeant

Title: Mask 1 —
(top left, bottom right
Client: Personal wor
Technique: Collag
200(

Title: Don't Cr
(top right
Technique: Collage
200(

Title: Yes Lov
(bottom left
Technique: Collage
200

Title: Twin Face 1—4
Technique: Collage
2007

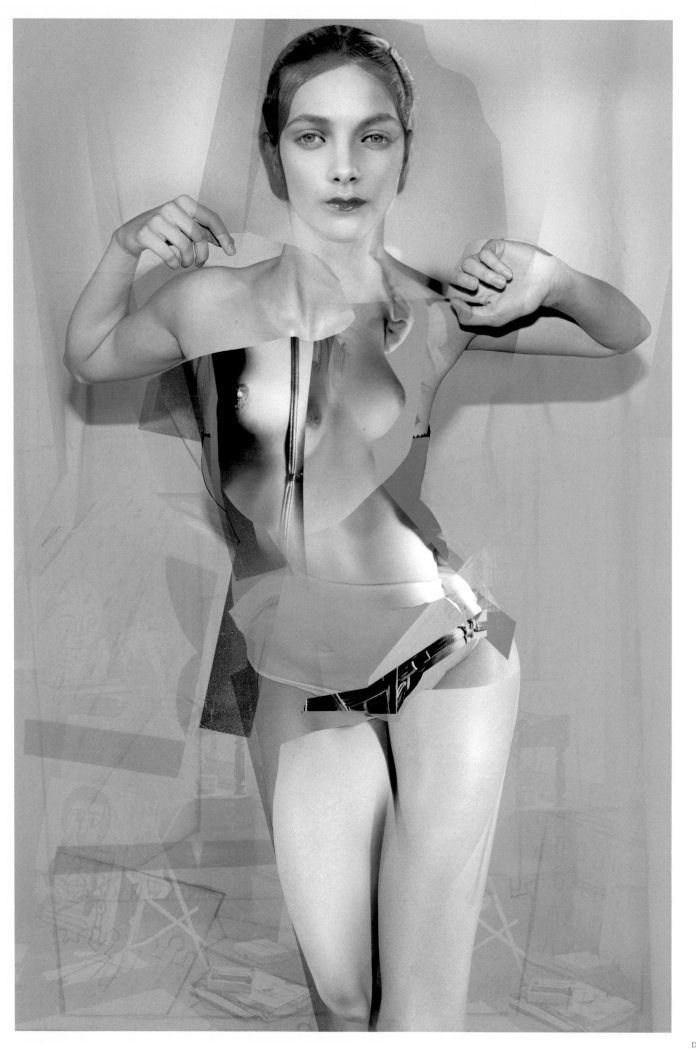

Ingrid Baars

Title: Olga Khokhlova—
Artist Lover Series
Technique:
Photography, Photoshop
2008

Ingrid Baars

Title: I'm No Angel—
Screen Siren Series
(top)
Client: DIF Magazine
Art Director: Pieter Schol
Stylist: Angela Kuperus
Make-up Artist: Ed Tijsen
Model: Stef, Maxmodels.nl
Format: Editorial
Photography, Photoshop
2008

Title: The Pleasure Garden
(bottom left)
Technique:
Photography, Photoshop
2008

Untitled
(bottom right)
Technique:
Photography, Photoshop
2008

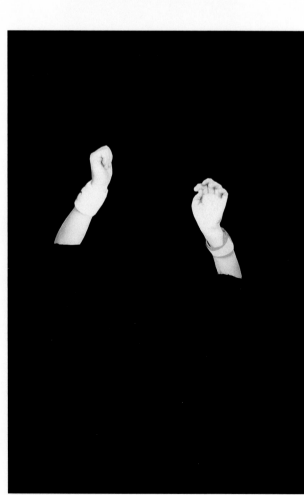

Made With Hate

Title: Der Krieg
(top left)
Technique: Collage
2009

Title: Just Like Dis
(top right)
Technique: Collage
2009

Title: Ghostly
(bottom left)
Technique: Collage
2009

Untitled
(bottom right)
Technique: Collage
2009

ContainerPLUS

Title: Dreamstory
(top + bottom)
Technique: Hand-drawn
illustration, photocopied
photography, mixed media
collage, elements all combined
and photographed
2009

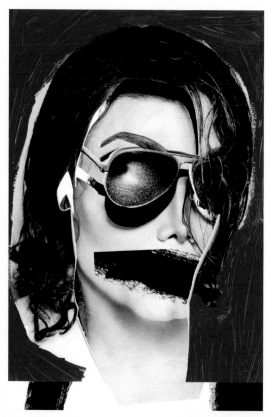

Paul Burgess

Title: Serge Gainsbourg
(top left)
Client: If You Could—Issue #2
Format: Editorial
Technique: Collage, digital
2007

Title: Taking the Michael
(top right)
Format: Exhibition
Technique:
Collage, paint, mixed media
2009

Title: Faith
(bottom)
Format: Exhibition
Technique:
Collage, mixed media, digital
2008

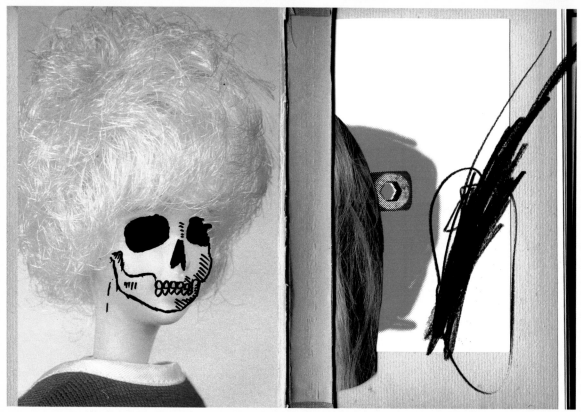

Matthew Rose

Title: A Perfect F=riend
(top left)
Format: Exhibition
Technique:
Collage on vintage paper
2003

Title: 12:05
(top right)
Format: Exhibition
Technique:
Collage on vintage paper
2004

Title: Le Mystere
(bottom left)
Format: Exhibition
Technique:
Collage on vintage photo.
2006

Title: Immaculate Perception
(bottom right)
Format: Exhibition
Technique:
Collage on vintage paper
2003

Paul Burgess

Title: Virchow-Seckel
(top left)
Format: Exhibition
Technique: Collage
2009

Title: Love You More
(top right)
Format: Exhibition
Technique:
Collage, mixed media, paint
2008

Title: Family
(bottom left)
Format: Exhibition
Technique:
Collage, mixed media, digital
2009

Title: The Horror
(bottom right)
Format: Exhibition
Technique: Collage
2009

Paul Burgess

Title: Snap
(top left)
Format: Exhibition
Technique: Collage / Digital
2009

Title: Red Dress Girl
(top right)
Format: Exhibition
Technique: Collage, mixed media
2009

Title: Blob Heads
(bottom left)
Format: Exhibition
Technique:
Collage, mixed media, digital
2009

Title: 45 King
(bottom right)
Format: Exhibition
Technique:
Collage, mixed media, digital
2009

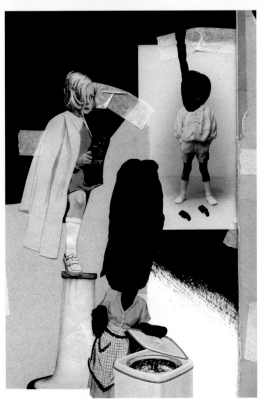

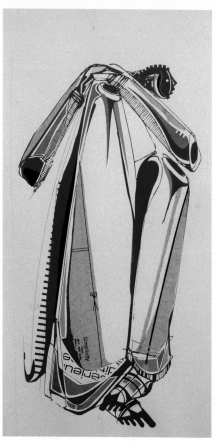

Amose

Untitled
(top left)
Technique: Hand-drawn,
Illustrator, Photoshop
2008

Title: Couple
(top right)
Technique: Ink, glued paper
2009

Untitled
(bottom left)
Technique: Screenprint on paper
2008

Untitled
(bottom centre)
Technique: Screenprint,
glued paper
2008

Title: Couple
(bottom right)
Technique: Ink, glued paper
2009

Amose

Untitled
(top left)
Technique: Ink on paper
2008

Untitled
(top right)
Technique:
Ink on paper, glued paper
2008

Untitled
(bottom left)
Technique: Ink on paper
2008

Untitled
(bottom right)
Technique: Hand-drawn,
Illustrator, Photoshop
2006

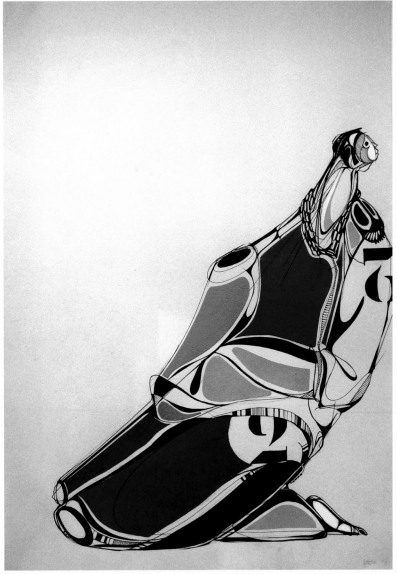

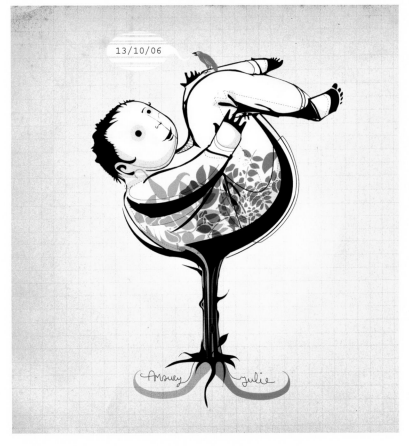

Raquel Aparicio

Title: Veronica's Etching at Seven
(top left)
Client: Madriz
Art Director: Vicente Ferrer
Format: Editorial
Technique: Hand-drawn, ink,
golden interference, digital
2009

Denise van Leeuwen

Title: Hahahaha!
Client: Nalden.net
Format: Wallpaper
(top right)

Title: Vraag & Antwoord
(bottom left)
Client: Rails
Format: Magazine cover

Title: Ziet Zitten
(bottom right)

All images:
Technique: Hand-drawn,
Photoshop
2008/9

Marco Marella

Title: Bastarono i Nostri 15 Anni
(top left)
Client: Baldini castoldi dalai editore
Art Director: Mara Scanavino
Format: Book cover
Technique: Mixed
2009

Title: Learning Languages
(top right)
Client: Hour Detroit Magazine
Art Director: Jessica Decker
Format: Editorial
Technique: Mixed
2009

Title: Latte, Solfato e Alby
Starvation
(bottom left)
Client: Baldini castoldi dalai editore
Art Director: Mara Scanavino
Format: Book cover
Technique: Mixed
2009

Title: The Return of Electroshock
as a Medical Treatment
(bottom right)
Client: The Village Voice
Art Director: L. D. Beghtol
Format: Editorial
Technique: Mixed
2008

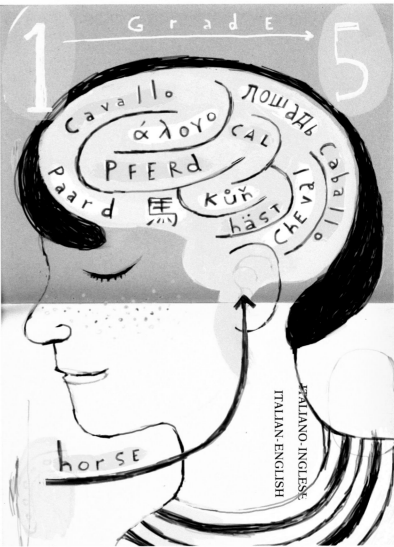

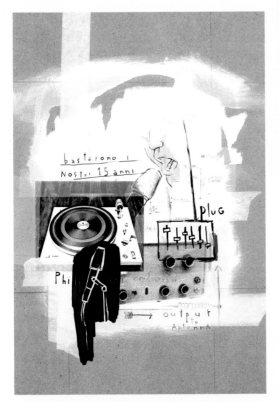

Towards Painting

There is no cutting corners in this chapter: blessed with a healthy dose of obsessive genius, the wilful talents assembled here have perfected traditional illustration techniques—and taken them that decisive step further, into the realm of narration, figurative painting and l'art pour l'art.

With a keen eye for both detail and composition, they slave away over just the right gradient, over endless patterns, structures and landscapes. Between masterful strokes of dizzying complexity, between paint and pencil, figure and fable, they carve out scenic realms of their own making that thrive on the dichotomy between classic craft and contemporary themes. Their uniting feature? The sheer quality of execution.

Rarely a mere, straightforward depiction, these richly personal interpretations take us to the world of Master and Margarita, of magic realism and rewritten identity.

Caught up in this dreamlike twilight zone, the resulting evocative visual tales take a leaf out of lowbrow painting or high art and splice them with slivers of pop or tongue-in-cheek detours to bygone techniques.

Here, zombified fairies meet copperplate creatures, while the iconic scoundrels of the Barricade game reveal an interest in retro-futurism. Detached from their original intent, we are treated to a subjective, even surreal slant on contemporary life.

Blessed with a true narrator's touch, these self-contained images tell it all. Sometimes encrypted, yet always accessible and open to interpretation, they spoil us with visual (hi)stories that not only describe their predefined subject, but work as equal, independent displays of skill and a seething imagination. Let's follow them to the outer limits of illustration, its precarious borders to fine art, and beyond.

Marco Wagner

Title: Fett im Hirn
Client: Effilee
Art Director: Heinz Elpermann
Format: Editorial
Technique:
Hand-drawn, Photoshop
2008

Marco Wagner

Title: Kartoffe
(top left
Client: Effilee
Art Director: Heinz Elpermann
Format: Editoria
Technique
Hand-drawn, Photoshop
2008

Title: Umzingel
(top right
Client: Effilee Magazin
Art Director: Heinz Elpermann
Picture Editor: Bettina Gosch
Format: Editorial
Technique
Hand-drawn, Photoshop
2009

Title: Zwei /
(bottom left)
Technique
Hand-drawn, Photoshop
2008

Title: Der Geist ist eine Gazelle
(bottom right)
Client: Effilee Magazin
Art Director: Heinz Elpermann
Picture Editor: Bettina Gosch
Format: Editorial
Technique:
Hand-drawn, Photoshop
2009

Marco Wagner

Title: Retter
(top left)
Curator: Mark Murphy
Format:
Painting for KNOW Exhibition
Technique: Acrylic on board
2008

Title: Java Affen
(top right)
Client: Playboy Germany
Art Director: Wolfgang Buß
Format: Editorial
Technique:
Hand-drawn, Photoshop
2009

Title: Jubiläum
(bottom upper left)
Client: Jutta Fricke
Format: Editorial
Technique:
Hand-drawn, Photoshop
2009

Title: Miller's
(bottom left)
Technique: Acrylic on board
2008

Title: Skorpionsfliegen
(bottom right)
Client: Playboy Germany
Art Director: Wolfgang Buß
Format: Editorial
Technique:
Hand-drawn, Photoshop
2009

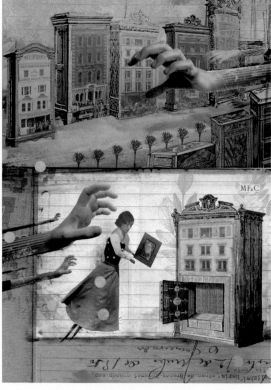

Lars Henkel

Title: Wasserwirtschaft
(top left)
Client:
Energieversorgung Mittelrhein
Format: Editorial
Technique: Collage
2008

Title: Nadja
(top right)
Client: Merck Finck & Co
Format: Editorial
Technique: Collage
2008

Title: Profil
(bottom left)
Client: Merck Finck & Co
Format: Editorial
Technique: Collage
2008

Title: Personalbericht
(bottom right)
Client:
Energieversorgung Mittelrhein
Format: Editorial
Technique: Collage
2008

Lars Henkel

Title: Einblick
(top left)
Client: Merck Finck & Co
Format: Editorial
Technique: Collage
2008

Title: Erdgasversorgung
(top right)
Client:
Energieversorgung Mittelrhein
Format: Editorial
Technique: Collage
2008

Title: Cover Vögel
(bottom left)
Client:
Energieversorgung Mittelrhein
Format: Editorial
Technique: Collage
2008

Title: Jahresabschluss
(bottom right)
Client:
Energieversorgung Mittelrhein
Format: Editorial
Technique: Collage
2008

Kristiana Pärn

Title: Baby Bir
(top left)
Format: Fine ar
Technique
Acrylic, pencil on woo
200

Title: Napping o
Marshmallow Branche
(top right)
Format: Fine ar
Technique
Acrylic, pencil on woo
2009

Title: Where Are You Fox?
(bottom left)
Format: Fine ar
Technique
Acrylic, pencil on woo
2007

Title
The Fox and the Marshmallow
(bottom right)
Format: Fine ar
Technique
Acrylic, pencil on woo
2008

Kristiana Pärn

Title: Rabbits in Vermillion
(top left)
Format: Fine art
Technique:
Acrylic, pencil on wood
2008

Title: Solitude
(top right)
Format: Fine art
Technique: Acrylic on wood
2008

Title: Barn
(bottom left)
Format: Fine art
Technique:
Acrylic, pencil on wood
2007

Title: Somersaults on Egg Hill
(bottom right)
Format: Fine art
Technique:
Acrylic, pencil on wood
2007

Interview Olaf Hajek

Touch, tactility and perception play a major part in Olaf 's richly coloured and textured illustrations. Whether animal-headed ladies of the night or Alice in Wonderland-like tableaux—the German painter's own flavour of "magic realism" might dress chubby cherubs in Mexican wrestler masks, but in his deliberate juxtaposition of fact and fiction, of plane and perception, Hajek forces his audience to take a leap of faith and shift their own perspective instead.

Background

I started drawing and painting at a very early age. At school, I took an oil painting class where they taught us to paint with our fingers. This really helped me to develop a strong artistic sense and a great feel for colour. I went on to study graphic design, and although illustration was not on the curriculum, I tried to draw as much as possible.

After graduation, I moved to Amsterdam where I would paint, make copies of my work and send them out to magazines. This is how the whole thing started. Looking back, I have worked as an illustrator for almost seventeen years. After a number of prestigious editorial assignments, they invited me to New York for a round of meetings with magazines like the New Yorker—a great experience!

Skills and techniques

I never studied illustration, but I took a few drawing classes while still at school. In my work, I apply acrylic paint to cardboard or wood and try to add a lot of texture. Later on, I paint the individual elements of the illustration onto this textured surface.

Inspiration and influences

I have always found inspiration in American folk art and Indian miniatures, African art and Mexican paintings, exploring the dichotomy between imagination and reality. I started out with a very expressive, darker palette that many clients found problematic. So, in the beginning I did not have a lot of mainstream clients, but over the years my style evolved into a more realistic and sometimes very colourful direction, without losing its characteristic naivety or folkloristic touch.

Not to forget that I am a painter and do not work with digital tools. Feeling the paint, touching its surface and working on it remains one of my biggest pleasures in life. Naturally, working for clients around the world and receiving wonderful feedback is also a great gift.

Work and play

One of the greatest things about being an illustrator is the sheer diversity of subjects and assignments. Right now, I am working on a series called "Revolution and Hair" for a cosmetics client, then there is a yoga book for children and an upcoming window installation for a New York gallery. I love the thematic variety, but I always stay true to my own style. In addition, I have started to spend a lot more time on my personal paintings—which in turn leave their mark on my commercial work.

Olaf Hajek

Title: Smell
Client: SZ Magazin
Art Director: Ludwig Wendt
Format: Editorial
Technique:
Acrylic on cardboard
2008

Olaf Hajek

Title: Natureman 3
(top left)
Technique: Acrylic on wood
2009

Title: Natureman 1
(top right)
Client: Illustrative
Format: For group exhibition
Illustrative 2008
Technique: Acrylic on cardboard
2008

Title: German Fashion
(bottom left)
Client: Capital
Art Director: Pascal Mänder
Format: Editorial
Technique: Acrylic on cardboard
2009

Title: Adoleszenz
(bottom right)
Client: Illustrative
Format: For group exhibition
Illustrative 2008
Technique:
Acrylic on cardboard
2008

Olaf Hajek

Title: Flowerhead
(top left)
Client: Illustrative
Format: For group exhibition
Illustrative 2008
Technique: Acrylic on cardboard
2008

Title: Black Antoinette
(top right)
Client: Illustrative
Format: For group exhibition
Illustrative 2008
Technique: Acrylic on cardboard
2008

Title: Natureman 2
(bottom left)
Technique: Acrylic on wood
2009

Title: Welcome
(bottom right)
Client: Illustrative
Format: For group exhibition
Illustrative 2008
Technique: Acrylic on cardboard
2008

Martin Haake

Title: General
(top left)
Client: 3x3 magazine
Credits: Charles Hively
Format: Magazine cover
Technique: Mixed media
2008

Title: Billionaire
(top right)
Client: Gault Millau Magazin
Format: Editorial
Technique: Mixed media
2008

Title: Family
(bottom)
Client: Illustrative 08
Format: Exhibition
Technique: Painting, collage
2008

Martin Haake

Title: Tarot
(top left)
Client: Andreas Jacobs
Format: Advertising
Technique: Mixed media
2009

Title: Doctors
(top right)
Client: Mylife
Format: Editorial
Technique: Mixed media
2009

Title: Amazon Monster I
(bottom)
Client: Ideageneration, London
Format: Exhibition
Technique:
Painting, collage
2009

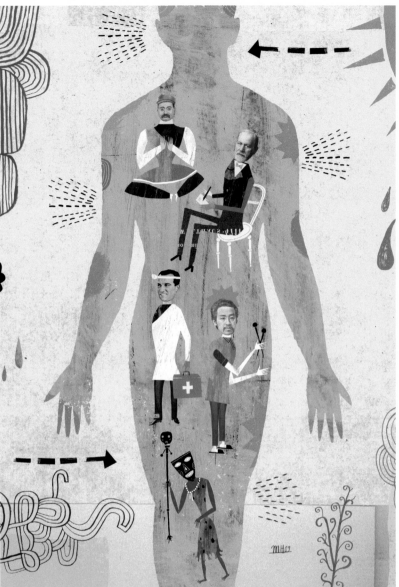

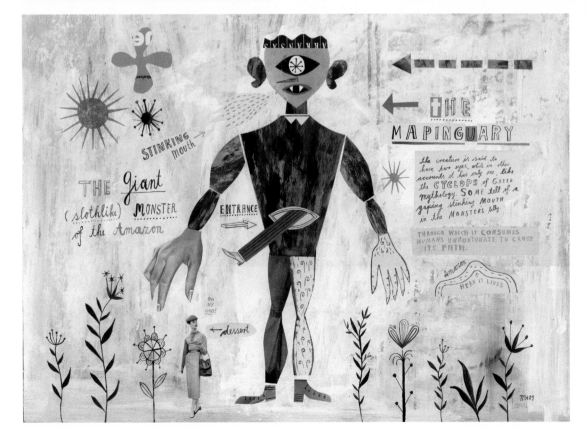

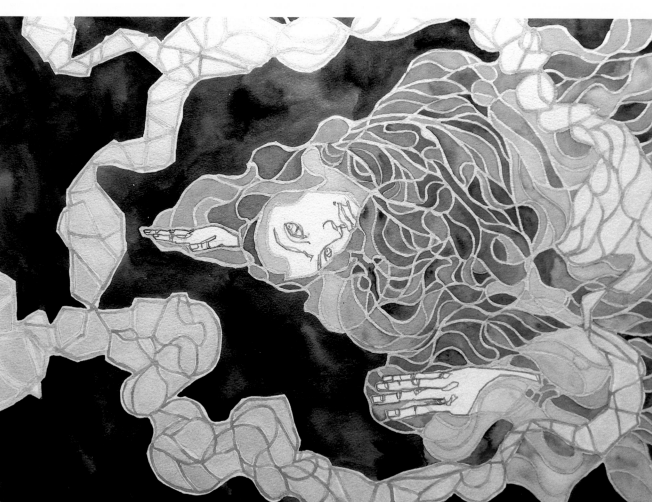

Hidetoshi Yamada

Title: Circle
(top)
Technique: Watercolour, ink
2004

Title: A Couple—Swirl / Cosmos
(bottom upper left)
Technique: Acrylic, silver glitter,
varnish, OHP film
on acrylic board
2007

Title: Hope
(bottom left bottom)
Technique: Acrylic on canvas
2007

Title: Pigmon
(bottom right)
Technique:
Watercolour on paper
1999

Viola Welker

Title: King Chameleon
with Choir 1
(top)
Technique: Acrylics, Indian ink
2008

Title: Human Behaviour
(bottom left)
Technique: Indian ink
2008

Title: Reminds 12
(bottom right)
Technique: Acrylic, Indian ink
on canvas
2008

Davide Zucco

Untitled
(top left)
Courtesy
Perugi artecontemporanea
Technique
Mixed media on leafs
2007

Title:
Amethyst Deceivers-Detail 02
(top right)
Courtesy
Perugi artecontemporanea
Technique:
Mixed media on leaf paper
2007

Title: Bleeding
(bottom)
Courtesy
Perugi artecontemporanea
Technique:
Mixed media on paper
2008

Davide Zucco

Title: EvilDevil
(top left)
Courtesy
Perugi artecontemporanea
Technique: Ink pen,
oil on golden paper
2005

Title: Amethyst Deceivers
(top right)
Courtesy
Perugi artecontemporanea
Technique:
Mixed media on leaf paper
2007

Title: Mask Bird Mali
(bottom left)
Courtesy
Perugi artecontemporanea
Technique: Mixed media on wood
2009

Title: Burning Colours Trying to
Turn My Blood Black
(bottom right)
Courtesy
Perugi artecontemporanea
Technique:
Mixed media on leaf paper
2007

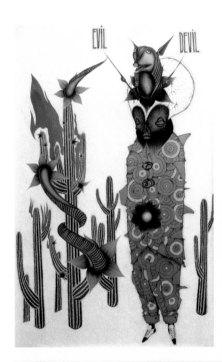

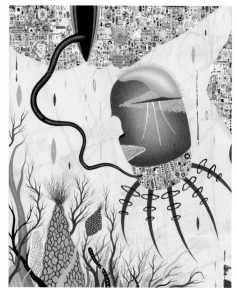

Colin Johnson

Title: Scorched Earth
(top left)
Client: Harvard Business Review
Art Director: Annette Trivette
Format: Editorial
Technique:
Mixed media on board
2007

Title: Born
(top right)
Client: Born Magazine
Art Director: Scott Benish
Format: Editorial
Technique:
Mixed media on wood
2007

Title: The Road
(bottom left)
Client: The Dallas Morning News
Art Director: Michael Hogue
Format: Editorial
Technique:
Mixed media on board
2006

Title: Going Nowhere
(bottom right)
Client: Plansponsor
Art Director: SooJin Buzelli
Format: Editorial
Technique:
Mixed media on board
2007

Colin Johnson

Title: Fringe Fest
(top left)
Client: City Pages
Art Director: Nick Vlcek
Format: Editorial
Technique:
Mixed media on board
2005

Title: Online Music Services
(top right)
Client: Chicago Tribune
Art Director: Hugo Espinoza
Format: Editorial
Technique:
Mixed media on board
2007

Title: Spring Shoe Guide
(bottom left)
Client: Runner's World
Art Director: Kory Kennedy
Format: Editorial
Technique:
Mixed media on board
2007

Title: Releasing The Brakes
(bottom right)
Client: Bike Magazine
Art Director: Shaun Bernadou
Format: Editorial
Technique:
Mixed media on board
2007

Russell Cobb

Title: The Fall
(top left)
Technique: Painting
2008

Title: Formula for Optimism
(top right)
Technique: Painting
2008

Title: Polar Bear
(bottom left)
Technique: Painting
2008

Title: The German Philosopher
(bottom right)
Technique: Painting
2008

Russell Cobb

Title: Fall From Grace
(top left)
Technique: Painting
2008

Title: The Collector
(top right)
Technique: Painting
2008

Title: The Walnut Tree
(bottom left)
Technique: Painting
2008

Title: The Mountain Climber
(bottom right)
Technique: Painting
2008

Anne Faith Nicholls

Title: Their Daily Bread
(top left)
Client: The SF Weekly
Format: Cover, Editorial
Technique: Acrylic on Paper
2009

Title: The Plunge
(top right)
Format: Fine art
Technique:
Oil, acrylic on canvas
2008

Title: The Prize Hunt
(bottom left)
Format: Fine art
Technique: Oil on canvas
2008

Title: Los Angeles Burning
(bottom right)
Technique: Acrylic on canvas
2008

Anne Faith Nicholls

Title: Escape
(top left)
Format: Editorial
Technique: Mixed media on paper
2009

Title: Seattle
(top right)
Format: For published book &
special project "S+imulus Package"
Technique: Acrylic on wood
2009

Title: Play Your Own Sad Songs
(bottom left)
Format: Fine art
Technique: Oil, acrylic on canvas
2008

Title: Checkout
(bottom right)
Format: Fine art
Technique: Oil, acrylic on canvas
2008

Alberto Cerriteño

Title: The Enamored Monkey
(top left)
Client: Artful Goods
Format: Exhibition
Technique: Digital
2009

Title: Lion
(top right)
Client: Personal
Format: Publishing
Technique: Digital
2009

Title: Tres
(bottom left)
Format: Print for sale
Technique: Digital
2008

Title: Yearning For Freedom
(bottom right)
Format: Print for sale
Technique: Digital
2009

Alberto Cerriteño

Title: Morbo
(top left)
Client: Complot Magazine
Format: Editorial
Technique: Acrylic, digital
2007

Title: The Enamored Owl
(top right)
Client: Gelaskins
Format:
Vinyl skin for electronic devices
Technique: Digital
2008

Title: Lolo Meditating
(bottom left)
Client: Zupi Magazine
Format: Editorial
Technique: Digital
2007

Title: Recuerdos
(bottom right)
Client: Hello Seahorse
Format: Record sleeve
Technique: Digital
2009

Lisel Ashlock

Title: Pelicans
(top left)

Title: A Confederate General
(top right)

Title: Narcissism
(bottom left)

Title: Tree
(bottom right)

All images:
Technique: Acrylic on wood
2009

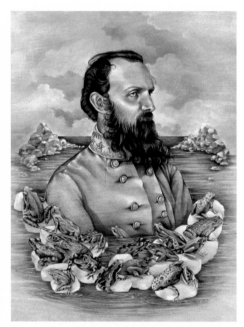

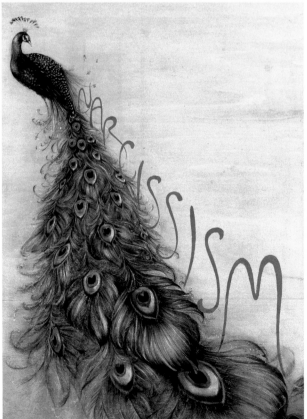

Lisel Ashlock

Title: Cathy (Kate)
(top left)

Title: Hysteria
(top right)

Title: Obsession and Phobias
(bottom left)

Title: Love
(bottom right)

All images:
Technique: Acrylic on wood
2009

Yoko Furusho

Title: Melancholy of
a Japanese Girl
(top left)
Client: Dpi magazine
Format: Editorial
Technique: Ink, acrylic
2008

Title: Treasure
(top right)
Client: Planadviser magazine
Format: Editorial
Technique: Ink, acrylic
2008

Title: Health-Virus
(bottom)
Client: LP and P
Format: Fine art
Technique: Ink, acrylic
2008

Yoko Furusho

Title: Royal Hunter
(top left)
Format: Children's book
Technique: Ink, acrylic
2008

Title: Bells and Whistles
(top right)
Client:
Plansponsor magazine
Format: Editorial
Technique: Ink, acrylic
2008

Title: The Pool of Tears
of Alice in Wonderland
(bottom)
Format: Children's book
Technique:
Ink, acrylic
2008

Peter Hoffmann

Title: The Collected Adventures
of Dystopia Green
(top left — 2 images)
Client: Encore Magazine
Format: Editorial
Technique: Hand-drawn,
watercolour, digital
2008

Title: Please Devil,
Send Me Golden Hair
(top right)
Client: Bubonix
Format: Poster
Technique: Hand-drawn,
watercolour, digital
2008

Title: Zero Gravity
(bottom)
Client: Soapbox
Format: DVD sleeve
Technique: Hand-drawn,
watercolour, digital
2007

Ruth Munro

Title: Butterfly Net
(top left)
Technique: Ink, digital
2008

Title: Plunger
(top upper right)
Technique: Ink, digital
2008

Title: Climbing
(top lower right)
Technique: Ink, digital
2008

Title: Carny
(bottom)
Technique: Ink, digital
2008

Amy Sol

Title: Migration
(top)
Technique:
Acrylic on wood panel
2008

Title: Flying fish
(bottom left)
Technique:
Acrylic on wood panel
2008

Title: Dust wings
(bottom right)
Technique:
Acrylic on wood panel
2008

Amy Sol

Title: It Becomes Lucid at Dusk
(top)
Technique:
Acrylic on wood panel
2008

Title: Sleeping Smoke
(bottom left)
Technique: Acrylic on wood panel
2008

Title:
We Found Ourselves Being Dreamt
(bottom right)
Technique:
Acrylic on wood panel
2008

Tadashi Ur

Title: Scenery of Japan
(top left + right)

Title: Soul of Mother
(bottom)

All images
Client: Tadaya
Technique (all)
Pencil, Photoshop
2007

Tadashi Ura

Title: 11 Messages
(left)
Technique: Pencil, Photoshop
2007

Title: Hydrangea
(right)
Technique: Indian ink, pencil,
Photoshop
2009

冥想続地冥合
覚醒十一諸湧出、回
有露睡境希掌
三天八番新官

Dopludo

Title: Natural Death
(top)
Technique: Digital
2008

Title: Frosted Coffee
(bottom left)
Technique: Digital
2008

Title: Cacao
(bottom right)
Technique: Digital
2008

Title: VO 1 + 2
(top)
Client: Valérie Oualid
Format: Advertising
Technique:
Photoshop, photography
2008

Title: Berger 1 + 2
(bottom)
Client:
The Ocean Doesn't Want Me
Format: Band graphics
Technique:
Photoshop, photography
2008

BERGER 1 crow
non drip gloss. no undercoat required.

BERGER 2 hummingbird
non drip gloss. no undercoat required.

Interview Yuko Shimizu

Yuko Shimizu takes her Asian roots and marries them to Western pop culture. In her rich illustrations, modern-day samurai and sassy geishas take traditional Japanese formalism out of its comfort zone and into the realm of contemporary consumerism. Between fact and (science) fiction, Abraham Lincoln and Angelina Jolie, illustration and fine art, the New Yorker has found her wilful niche—one she strives to escape with delightful regularity.

Background

I was one of those kids in your class who never went outside for lunch, but just stayed in the empty classroom to draw. Nevertheless, I majored in business. My family was very traditional and my parents did not want me to pursue something so "impractical". I ended up getting a job in a Japanese firm, doing PR for eleven years. During this time, my desire for art kept growing and growing. I had also gone to middle school in New York and wanted to return to where I felt I belonged. In 1999, I finally crossed the Pacific to start art college in New York—along with a bunch of 18-year-old freshmen. When you are almost twice as old, knowing that this is your second chance, you end up working three times as hard. In 2003, I graduated with an MFA in illustration.

I picked illustration because I was really interested in commercial art. During my time in advertising and PR, I had always been on the client side, nursing my secret jealousy for the illustrators I was working with, and I wanted to explore the other side.

Inspiration and influences

I do not really believe in "style"—style is just what is on the surface. What matters is your "personal voice", which in turn affects your style. Style may change over the years, as you grow as a person and as an artist, and it is also firmly anchored in time. Your personal voice, on the other hand, defines the core of who you are and how you want to express yourself.

So far I have accumulated many, many influences over the course of my life. When I was a kid in Japan during the 1960s and 1970s, my first drawings were influenced by animations and comics. I can still sense these in my work. Nowadays, when people ask me what my influences are, I say "everything I have experienced in my life", which seems very broad, but is basically true—good and bad, likes and dislikes, joy and pain.

Skills and techniques

At art school, they teach you the basics of drawing and painting, but the most important thing I learnt was to find out about myself. This may sound weird, but it was like a four-year therapy session. And I loved it. Anyway, once you know the basics, you can simply teach yourself. I use calligraphy brushes and Indian ink on watercolour paper, then scan the drawings to Photoshop and colour them digitally. Over the years—and by trial and error—I have developed my own, distinct way of colouring, but it still changes from one day to the next. You only learn when you make mistakes. It is part of life.

Work and play

As my work is, well, kind of odd, I only get calls from clients who know I am the right person for the job. This suits me just fine, as I am not interested in changing my approach or imitating someone else.

Almost all the artwork in this book was commissioned by ad agencies, publishers, magazines and newspapers.

I get bored if there is not enough variety in my work, so I tend to have a number of different jobs or themes happening at once. When I am in New York, it feels like I never escape my work, although I love it. In order to keep my creations fresh, I constantly require new input. By communicating with other artists, students and aspiring illustrators, I get so much back in return! I also love travelling and taking public transport in foreign countries. Each city has its own logic and I learn a great deal about different cultures and common sense.

Yuko Shimizu

Title: Nightmare
Client: Bostonia Magazine
Art Director: Ronn Campisi
Format: Editorial
Technique: Ink, Photoshop
2009

Yuko Shimizu

Title: Letters of Desire
All images:
Format: Book project
Technique: Ink, Photoshop
2002

Yuko Shimizu

Title: Measuring A Bear
(top)
Client: Plansponsor Magazine
Art Director: SooJin Buzelli
Format: Editorial
Technique: Ink, Photoshop
2008

Title:
Tiger Beer Advertising (1 of 2)
(bottom)
Client: CHI & Partners, Tiger Beer
Format: Billboard advertising
Technique: Ink, Photoshop
2008

Dennis Juan Ma

Title: Powerful Tiger
Format: Exhibition
Technique: Pencil, ink, digital
2008

Dennis Juan Ma

Title: Grace 2
(top left)
Client: Dale Cusack
Format: Book cover
Technique: Pencil, ink, digital
2008

Title: Grace 1
(top right)
Client: Dale Cusack
Format: Book cover
Technique: Pencil, ink, digital
2008

Title: Warrior
(bottom left)
Format: Exhibition
Technique: Pencil, ink, digital
2008

Title: Voyage
(bottom right)
Client: Tiger Beer
Format: Tiger Translate
exhibition poster
Technique: Pencil, ink, digital
2008

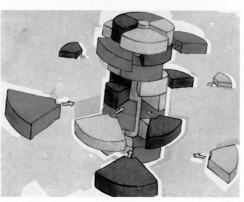

Elliott Golden

Title: Fighting Health Bills
(top left)
Client: Body + Soul Magazine
Credits: Asya Palatova
Format: Editorial
Technique: Acrylic, digital
2008

Title: Overpaid CEOs
(top right)
Client:
University of Pennsylvania Gazette
Credits: Catherine Gontarek
Format: Editorial
Technique: Acrylic, digital
2009

Title: Risky Business
(bottom upper left)
Client:
Institutional Investor Magazine
Credits: Jennifer Klock
Format: Editorial
Technique: Acrylic, digital
2009

Title: Data Management
(bottom lower left)
Client:
Institutional Investor Magazine
Credits: Anthony Scerri
Format: Editorial
Technique: Acrylic, digital
2008

Title: Dream
(bottom right)
Client:
The Secret Language of Dreams
Credits: Suzanne Tuhrim
Format: Book
Technique: Acrylic, digital
2009

Ian Kim

Title: Exiles on Main Street
(top left)
Client: Koream
Art Director: Corina Knoll
Format: Editorial
Technique:
Graphite, acrylic, digital
2007

Title: Flight
(top right)
Client: Nike Women
Company: Buck
Format:
Motion graphics style frame
Technique:
Graphite, acrylic, digital
2008

Title: Heat
(bottom left)
Client: Runner's World
Art Director: Marc Kauffman
Format: Editorial
Technique:
Graphite, acrylic, digital
2007

Untitled
(bottom right)
Client: Education Week
Art Director: Gina Tomko
Format: Editorial
Technique:
Graphite, acrylic, digital
2007

Marcos Chin

Title: Elizabeth May,
Or May Not
(top left)
Client: More, Canada
Credits: Faith Cochran
Format: Editorial
Technique: Digital
2009

Title: Girl Gaming
(top right)
Client: Delta, Sky Magazine
Credits: Ann Harvey
Format: Editorial
Technique: Hand-drawn, digital
2008

Untitled
(centre)
Client: Dutch Uncle
Format: Wallet Design
Technique: Hand-drawn, digital
2009

Title: Jack and the Aktuals
(bottom left)
Client: Tor.com
Art Director: Irene Gallo
Format: Web
Technique: Hand-drawn, digital
2008

Title: What Are They
Doing To My School?
(bottom right)
Client:
The Boston Globe Magazine
Art Director: Emily Kehe
Format: Editorial
Technique: Hand-drawn, digital
2008

Maya Shleifer

Title: Hawaii Myth
(top)
Client: Zmora Beitan Publishing
Format: Book
Technique: Photoshop
2008

Title: Forest
(centre)
Client: "Masa Aher" magazine
Format: Editorial
Technique:
Hand-drawn, digital
2008

Kyung Soon Park

Title: Fishing For Answers
(bottom)
Client: The Globe & Mail
Art Director: Cinders Mcleod
Format: Editorial
Technique: Painted, digital
2008

Felix Gephart

Title: Survivor
Client: FSC
Format: Calendar
Technique: Pen, ink, digital
2009

Yuta Onoda

Title: Hope Leaves
(top upper left)

Title: The Mask She Wears
(top lower left)

Title: Restoring What is Lost
(top right)

Title: Please Me One More Time
(bottom)

All images:
Credits: Thomas Sevalrud
Format: Editorial
Technique:
Mixed media, digital
2009

Maya Shleifer

Untitled
(top left + right)
Technique: Mixed media
2008

Kyung Soon Park

Title: Hands Across the Water
(bottom left)
Client: More Magazine
Art Director: Faith Cochran
Format: Editorial
Technique: Painted
2008

Title: Work & Life
(bottom right)
Client: Uppercase Gallery
Format: Exhibition
Technique: Mixed media
2008

John Malloy

Title: Al Green: Soul Survivor
(top left)
Client: Dazed & Confused
Format: Editorial
Technique: Pen, ink, digital
2007

Title: Weight Loss
(top right)
Technique:
Oil paint, pen, ink, digital
2008

Title: Personal Digital Highway
(bottom upper left)
Client: BPM Magazine
Format: Editorial
Technique:
Acrylic, pen, ink, digital
2007

Title: Rash
(bottom lower left)
Technique:
Oil paint, pen, ink, digital
2007

Title: Kathleen Edwards
(bottom right)
Client: Paste Magazine
Format: Editorial
Technique:
Acrylic, pen, ink, digital
2008

Tomer Hanuka

Title: Jaw Breaker
(top left)
Client: Vertigo
Format: Cover (unpublished)
Technique: Mixed
2008

Title: From God's Mountain III
(top right)
Client: Rocket Society
Technique: Mixed
2009

Title: From God's Mountain I
(bottom left)
Client: Juxtapoz
Format: Cover
Technique: Mixed
2008

Title: From God's Mountain II
(bottom right)
Client: Fantagraphics
Format: Book
Technique: Mixed
2008

Tomer Hanuka

Title: Marquis de Sade
(top left)
Client: Penguin
Art Director: Pau Buckley
Format: Book cover
Technique: Mixed
2006

Title: Life of Pi
(top right)
Client: Times
Format: Book proposal
Technique: Mixed
2006

Title: No Fare No Well
(bottom left)
Client: Playboy
Format: Editorial
Technique: Mixed
2007

Title: Old Moab
(bottom right)
Client: Playboy
Format: Editorial
Technique: Mixed
2008

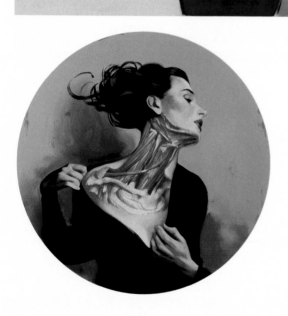

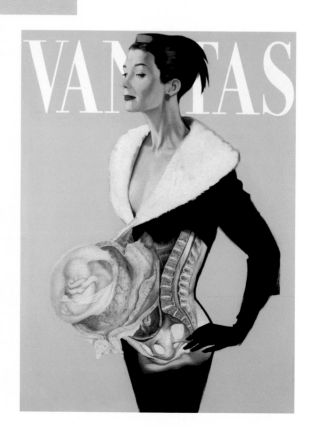

Fernando Vicente

Title: Máscara
(top left)

Title: Escorzo
(top upper right)

Title: Tornado
(top right centre)

Title: Iris
(top lower right)

Title: Interiores
(bottom left)

Title: Gravidez
(bottom right)

All images:
Technique:
Acrylic on canvas
2008

Fernando Vicente

Title: Maternidad
(top left)

Title: Beso sour
(top right)

Title: Dulce Porvenir
(bottom upper left)

Title: Humo
(bottom left centre)

Title: Presentimiento
(bottom lower left)

Title: Flor de piel
(bottom right)

All images:
Technique:
Acrylic on canvas
2008

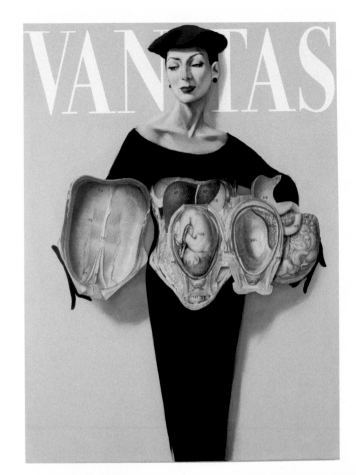

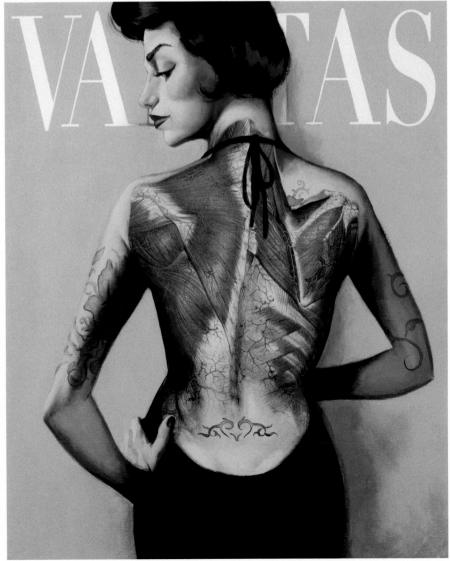

Ian Kim

Title: Exit Ghost
(top)
Client: Village Voice
Art Director: LD Beghtol
Format: Editorial
Technique:
Graphite, acrylic, digital
2007

Title: Guilty
(bottom left)
Technique:
Graphite, acrylic, digital
2007

Title: A Corpse in the Koryo
(bottom centre)
Client: Koream
Art Director: Corina Knoll
Format: Editorial
Technique:
Graphite, acrylic, digital
2007

Title: Hostage
(bottom right)
Client: Koream
Art Director: Corina Knoll
Format: Editorial
Technique:
Graphite, acrylic, digital
2007

Andrew Hem

Title: Madame Yellow
(top)
Technique: Oil on wood
2008

Title: Slow
(bottom left)
Technique: Oil on canvas
2008

Title: Left Behind
(bottom right)
Technique: Oil on wood
2008

Andrew Hem

Title: Befriend
(top left)
Technique: Oil on paper
2008

Title: Follow You in the Dark
(top right)
Technique: Oil on board
2008

Title: Blend In
(bottom)
Technique: Oil on wood
2008

Andrew Hem

Title: Fountain Blue
(top left)
Technique: Oil on Board
2008

Title: New Chapter
(top right)
Technique: Oil on canvas
2008

Title: North Station
(bottom)
Technique: Oil on wood
2008

Ana Bayagan

Title: Mildred
(top left)
Credits:
Collection of Danilo Rossi
Technique: Oil on panel
2009

Title: Chelsea
(top upper right)
Credits: Private Collection
Technique: Oil on panel
2009

Title: Cindy
(top lower right)
Credits:
Collection of Russel Wolke
Technique: Oil on panel
2009

Title: Esther
(bottom)
Credits:
Collection of Donna Baxter
Technique: Oil on panel
2009

Ana Bayagan

Title: Percy's Unlucky Day
(top upper left)
Credits:
Collection of John Purlia
Technique: Oil on panel
2009

Title: Water Birth
(top lower left)
Credits: Private Collection
Technique: Oil on panel
2009

Title: May—The Chrysalis
(top right)
Credits: Private Collection
Technique: Oil on panel
2009

Title: Guy List
(bottom)
Client: Men's Health Magazine
Format: Editorial
Technique: Oil on panel
2009

Illusive. Contemporary Illustration Part 3

Edited by Robert Klanten and Hendrik Hellige

Art Direction: Hendrik Hellige for Gestalten · Project Management: Julian Sorge for Gestalten · Production Management: Vinzenz Geppert for Gestalten
Cover Graphics: Petra Börner · Chapter Introductions & Interviews: Sonja Commentz · Preface: Claudia Mareis & Reinhard Wendler · Proofreading: Patricia Goren
Printed by Optimal Maedia Production GmbH, Röbel
Made in Germany

Published by Gestalten, Berlin 2009
ISBN: 978-3-89955-250-8
2nd printing, 2010

For more information, please visit www.gestalten.com

Bibliographic information published by the Deutsche Nationalbibliothek. The Deutsche Nationalbibliothek lists this publication in the Deutsche Nationalbibliografie; detailed bibliographic data is available on the internet at http://dnb.d-nb.de.

None of the content in this book was published in exchange for payment by commercial parties or designers; Gestalten selected all included work based solely on its artistic merit.

This book was printed according to the internationally accepted FSC standards for environmental protection, which specify requirements for an environmental management system.

Gestalten is a climate-neutral company and so are our products. We collaborate with the non-profit carbon offset provider myclimate (www.myclimate.org) to neutralize the company's carbon footprint produced through our worldwide business activities by investing in projects that reduce CO_2 emissions (www.gestalten.com/myclimate).